T5-CQB-125

THE SUCCESSFUL TEACHING SERIES

PRESCHOOL:
THE HUGGABLE
LEARNERS

LAWRENCE O. RICHARDS, PH.D.

David C. Cook Publishing Co.
ELGIN, ILLINOIS/WESTON, ONTARIO

Acknowledgments

Appreciation is due Elsiebeth McDaniel, specialist in Christian education of young children, author, and consultant, for her contribution to this work.

Note: The first edition of this book appeared under the title, *You and Your Preschooler.*

Scripture quotations, unless otherwise noted, are from the *Holy Bible: New International Version,* © 1973, 1978, 1984 by the New York International Bible Society, used by permission of Zondervan Bible Publishers.

Published by David C. Cook Publishing Co.
850 N. Grove Ave., Elgin, IL 60120
Cable address: DCCOOK

Designer: Dawn Lauck
Cover illustration: Jane Conteh-Morgan
Printed in U.S.A.
Library of Congress Catalog Card Number: 87-65366
ISBN: 1-55513-187-5

Contents

CHAPTER ONE
TOO YOUNG TO LEARN?

▶"Let the little children come to me, and do not hinder them, for the kingdom of God belongs to such as these. I tell you the truth, anyone who will not receive the kingdom of God like a little child will never enter it" (Mk. 10:14, 15).

Two-year-old Sarah lies on her back in the tub, gurgling with delight at the feel of the water. Four-year-old Josh watches the Nickelodeon cable TV channel for a few minutes, then wanders into his room to play with blocks before deserting them for GI Joes. Three-year-old Matt snuggles up to Mom, watching as she reads a story he's heard a thousand times.

Watch the same children playing together in church or preschool, and it may seem to be chaos. Two boys want the same truck. A girl howls when another child grabs a crayon on the table near her. Even older preschoolers, who sit side by side cutting a take-home project, don't seem to play together. Each is involved in his or her own activity. Yet each seems so easily distracted by what others do, so ready to leave a task unfinished when attracted to something new.

THE HUGGABLE LEARNERS

Some adults aren't used to thinking of preschoolers as persons who can, and who need to, *learn*. All too often these youngest of our children are viewed as having no real capabilities or needs; they're just youngsters to care for until they grow old enough to sit still and be taught.

Yet the fact is that during these preschool years some of the most significant learning of all takes place!

1. *Preschoolers learn language.* They learn the meaning of simple words first. But soon they're putting words together in sentences. A two-year-old learns, and experiments with, the power of "No!" Threes and fours ask question after question, often driving moms and dads to distraction. By the time a child reaches age five, letters take on meaning. And many a child who has just turned five takes great joy in counting.

I remember a Mauldin cartoon from the Second World War (yes, I'm really *that* old!), in which GI Joe, commenting on young French children, says with wonder to a buddy, "Gee, how'd they learn to speak a foreign language so young?" The joke seemed funny, of course, because we all knew how they learned a "foreign" language. They grew up with parents and friends who spoke French, and the language wasn't foreign to them. Even the learning wasn't foreign. These boys and girls learned the language, as almost every person does, by hearing it and practicing it *as preschoolers.* Yet language is one of the most difficult and complicated things any human being can learn!

2. *Preschoolers learn relationships.* Watch a boy or girl who is playing or who is fastened to the TV and observing Sesame Street. Watch while Mom, working in the kitchen, calls, "Suzie, come to the table." Chances are Suzie will stay right where she is, totally ignoring Mom's call. Mom will call again a couple of

times. And then, in a much sterner voice, she'll say, "Suzie, come to the table!" and *then* Suzie will respond. Our three-year-old already knows the difference between Mom's "come on" voice and her "COME ON!" voice.

Preschoolers learn to pick up even subtle clues in the voice or appearance of the important adults that constitute their worlds. Most moms have been surprised, when feeling especially tired or down, to have their three year olds come over, put a hand on an arm and say sympathetically, "Don't feel bad, Mommy."

3. *Preschoolers learn many skills.* Toilet training is one—but just one. Preschoolers learn to walk. They learn to put on and take off clothes. They learn how to eat at the table and use the correct utensils. They learn how to turn the TV on and off, get the paper for Dad, buckle their seat belts, and a host of other things. They learn to hold crayons and color. They learn to draw people as more than stick figures with giant heads and spindly arms and legs. They learn to recognize colors and sort objects according to size and shape.

4. *Preschoolers learn patterns.* Patterns are important in all our lives. We get up and go to bed, we eat, we organize our weeks according to regular patterns. Preschoolers soon learn the patterns, too. They know when Saturday comes and they can climb in bed with Mom or Dad for hugs. They know when it's mealtime, and in Christian homes they know that folding or holding hands and thanking God for food is part of the regular pattern of living. They like bedtime rituals—reading, songs, a good-night prayer to memorize. They know that Sunday is a special day with special clothes and church to look forward to.

5. *Preschoolers learn social skills.* It may seem hard

to believe when we see two youngsters tugging at the same doll, but it's true. Preschoolers can learn that others exist and have rights. They learn the magic phrase, "I had it first," and that establishes their claim to a debated toy. They learn to take turns. Somehow it begins to seem fair to a preschooler when Dad says, "We'll set the timer for 10 minutes, Josh. You can have the truck till the timer rings, and then Ken gets 10 minutes."

Young preschoolers play in parallel, not really *with* but *beside* others. Yet during these few years they'll learn cooperative play: sharing toys, taking turns, building a castle together instead of side by side.

So, before we dismiss these preschool years as not all that important, let's consider:

Preschoolers learn language.

Preschoolers learn relationships.

Preschoolers learn skills.

Preschoolers learn patterns.

Preschoolers learn social skills.

Some of the most important learning we do will, and must, take place during the preschool years! How important, then, that we think seriously about the Christian nurture of preschoolers. For God has a place in every life—even, as Jesus pointed out, in the life of the "little child."

Foundations for Faith

Christie was afraid. She was all alone in her dark bedroom, and everyone else was downstairs. So she began to sing a Sunday School song, "Jesus Is with Me All Through the Night."

Next Sunday, as Christie told her class what had happened, it was clear that Jesus really had helped her fall asleep. Jesus had been very real and present with

Christie through a song she'd learned at church. How tragic it would have been if Christie's parents had decided to wait to bring Christie to church until she was "old enough to learn"!

The mother of ten-month-old Jason began having a quiet time with him each afternoon before his nap. Mom didn't pray long prayers, but she did sing a hymn and hold Jason's hands while she prayed briefly. By the time Jason was 15 months old he was bowing his head in imitation of his mother. Before he was two years old, Jason was talking to God, praying in his own words.

Too many people who worry about the teen years fail to realize that all the years up to 13 help make a child what he is. The foundations for faith are laid early. A child who learns trust in childhood, and whose thoughts in times of stress turn to God, is going to be a relatively stable teen. It's true that some teens with good foundational teaching do rebel, yet God's promise remains. If we "Train a child in the way he should go, and when he is old he will not turn from it" (Prov. 22:6).

Moms, dads, and adults who minister to preschoolers in church and Christian day schools can help lay the foundations for lifelong faith—if they provide the nurture our youngest children need.

Given the fact that children learn so many things during the preschool years, we need to ask *how* they learn. The answer to that question is basic in our whole approach to teaching our youngest boys and girls. The answer is established in a fascinating Bible passage, Deuteronomy 6:5-7. These words of Moses are addressed to parents, but are also basic for anyone who seeks to teach spiritual truths:

Love the Lord your God with all your heart and with all your soul and with all your strength.

These commandments that I give you today are to be upon your hearts. Impress them on your children. Talk about them when you sit at home and when you walk along the road, when you lie down and when you get up.

The pattern we see here describes what is to happen both in the home and in the church where preschoolers are taught. Note the following elements.

1. The parents (adults) love God. Out of this love they create a context in which God's love is lived out. Thus young boys and girls have the chance to learn about God in a setting which mirrors God's own qualities and His character.

2. The words of God, which explain the way the adults live, are talked about with the children. The imagery here is not so much of formal teaching but of informal. Adults simply talk about God and His Word as they would talk about other things with the boys and girls.

3. The talk takes place in a flow of shared experiences. Again the setting is not a formal classroom, but rather "when you sit at home and when you walk along the road, when you lie down and when you get up." Guiding everyday experiences and turning thoughts to God is the key to teaching preschoolers, and to a large extent to teaching older children.

For a more thorough explanation of the implications of this important Biblical concept, see another book in this series, *Parents: Round-the-Clock Teachers.* For an explanation of how to apply this concept in teaching preschoolers, read *this* book!

Summing Up
The preschool years are the longest period when a child

will believe anything, is most dependent, is learning the most, and is also undergoing rapid physical and mental development. These are the years when a child is gaining control over his or her environment primarily through the senses, and is trying to integrate and assimilate what he or she sees, hears, feels, and even tastes. Is it important for Christian adults to help guide the child in these experiences? During these believing years, a child is trying to fit pieces together and understand the world in which he or she lives. How very important it is for that child to find the Creator and Sustainer of the things that arouse his or her curiosity and wonder! A young child marvels at the travels of a dandelion seed, the soft fur of a kitten, and a duck's ability to dive. As the child grows in appreciation of God and all He has made, he or she may respond in the words of one four-year-old: "Isn't God clever?"

If you are to teach preschoolers, you must have a good Sunday School curriculum that takes into account the growth of children—not only physical, but mental and spiritual. Only since about 1960 has there been much concern in the church about preschoolers. Even so, many of the early programs for nursery children were similar to those of secular kindergartens. Teachers did not have Biblical curriculums, so they patterned their teaching after the public kindergarten, injecting a few Bible verses "to keep the lessons spiritual." We now know, however, that children under six are ready for many spiritual truths.

Today, Christian education recognizes the growth patterns of young children. Through recognizing normal development, we are better prepared to teach the whole child and to pace the Sunday School program to his or her needs and abilities.

In teaching a preschooler spiritual truths, you must: (1) help a child find meaning where he or she is right now; (2) lay foundations for conversion when the child reaches the age of accountability; and (3) provide a foundation for the child's continuing growth and service as a Christian. In teaching preschoolers, you show God's love and how He expects His people to live. A few children may be able to understand salvation and receive Christ as Savior (see Chapter 4 for a detailed discussion of salvation and conversion). Many preschoolers, however, require more time to realize their need of a Savior.

Should you become unduly concerned about the age of accountability? Is every child accountable at the same age?

We may as well ask whether every four-year-old exhibits the same manual dexterity, or whether all five-year-old boys are the same height. Of course, you are deeply concerned about teaching children to respond to God as they are ready. By teaching how God expects His people to obey Him and to treat others, you are also explaining a standard which, sooner or later, thinking boys and girls will realize they cannot attain; they will need God's help.

If you did not teach the standards of Christian behavior, it is possible that children would never know what God expects of them and how He has provided for their salvation. If the love of God is reality, then it is part of a meaningful life. Preschoolers need to be introduced to His life in ways they can understand. If life is worthless without Jesus, then why not teach preschoolers something about life *with* Jesus?

Before a child becomes a Christian, you are helping him or her learn what standard of behavior is acceptable to God. This process begins even before a child is old enough to know what it means to receive Jesus Christ as Savior. When you teach young children God's truth, you are preparing the soil into which the seed, the Word of God, may take root and grow. Children who attend Sunday School during their early years—particularly children from Christian homes—are ready sooner to be led by the Holy Spirit to believe that Jesus loves them, is their Friend, and wants their love in return.

Through your teaching and the example of other Christians, the young child sees ways of thinking and acting in accordance with God's Word. By observing the actions of adults around him, the little child begins to recognize sharing, helping, being kind, and other expressions of love as patterns of life for those who love Jesus.

A child who receives Scriptural teaching develops a Biblical awareness of the world in which he or she lives. The child feels that life, people, and experiences are all part of God's loving plan and care. If the young child can believe early in God and count on His unconditional love for him or her as a person of worth, that child can begin to cope with life. He or she feels secure in the reality of God's unchanging love.

You cannot make a child into a Christian by trying to get his behavior to conform to Bible standards. But a young child who is familiar with what God's Word teaches is better prepared to become a Christian.

Why bother to teach preschoolers? Because God says, "Train up a child," and we who are His older children want to obey.

REACT

1. In your own experience, what makes teaching preschoolers important?

2. Can you think of other examples of preschool learning?

ACT

1. Children under six can be infuriating if you don't understand them. Want to make your work with them easier? Get to know these little people and you will make your own life more peaceful and your teaching more meaningful. Decide to read this book and apply its principles to your own teaching.

2. The teacher of young children recognizes that his or her own faith, beliefs, and attitudes become part of those children. Are you willing to have your beliefs become part of a child's life? Are there things you want to change?

CHAPTER TWO
THE IDEAL TEACHER

▶ "So then, just as you received Christ Jesus as Lord, continue to live in him, rooted and built up in him, strengthened in the faith as you were taught, and overflowing with thankfulness" (Col. 2:6, 7).

"Anyone can teach young children!" someone tells you. "After all, they are easily amused." How simply that person equates amusing children with teaching them! That person confuses *quiet* children with *learning* children; the two are not always the same.

If someone should ask you to teach preschoolers, saying how easy it will be because preschoolers can't learn much, would you agree? Not if you have read and believed Chapter 1! Those under six are some of the most important people anyone can ever teach.

Any man or woman who decides to teach preschoolers should realize that, first of all, he or she must have a vital relationship with Jesus Christ. Paul prayed for the Colossians, "That you may live a life worthy of the Lord and may please him in every way: bearing fruit in every good work, growing in the knowledge of God" (Col. 1:10). This Bible verse and the one at the beginning of the chapter offer an excellent description of a teacher—the believer who walks with God, is being built up in Him, and is increasing in the knowledge of the Lord.

A teacher must know the Lord intimately, believing in Him as personal Savior and growing in the knowledge of Him. To become a teacher should mean a calling from God and a dedication to Him for a special service. And when Christians teach because they love the Lord Jesus, that love is bound to show in love for others. We become persons who teach because we care about the people we teach—little children—and we care for them as individuals.

This chapter will help you discover qualities a preschool teacher needs to teach the children described in the next chapter. The rest of the book will tell you what preschoolers can learn and that they learn best through educational or structured play. The room, the materials, and the furniture are all part of the learning environment, but they are not the most important factor. You, the teacher, are the key to successful teaching and learning in the preschool departments of your Sunday School.

Because the teacher is the key to success, churches should want the very best qualified people. You, teacher, are the person who will reflect the Lord Jesus and His love for children under six.

Qualities to Cultivate

What makes a good preschool teacher? A number of Christian educators have developed lists of commandments for teachers, most of which are helpful in identifying the qualifications of a good preschool teacher. In addition to knowing the Lord Jesus, "A teacher must be a real man or woman," said early Christian educator Marion Lawrance. You can decide for yourself what he meant, but I believe he was saying that a teacher should be the highest and best example that any man or woman can be. Someone has said that throughout the years people have been looking for better methods, but God has been looking for better men and women.

The preschool teacher must believe in the Book he teaches and grow in his knowledge of it. He should read the Book and live it. The preschool lessons may contribute little additional Bible knowledge, so the teacher must make study a personal habit.

The best preschool teacher has genuine love for people. That love will be felt by both children and parents. The teacher will be sensitive to the needs of young children, remembering that during the church session, he or she is a substitute parent who may be called upon to make an imagined or real hurt "go away." The teacher knows when the problem of the moment demands a story or when to pray for a special need mentioned by the child. He or she knows when it is time to suggest a spontaneous activity because it fits the mood.

The teacher must believe in prayer, being ready to pray for himself or herself as well as for students. Martin Luther is credited with a thought that no Christian should forget:"I am so busy with so many things to attend to that I must spend at least three hours in prayer every day."

A preschool teacher must be willing to work and learn, because there will always be more to know about children. We are teaching living persons, and they will change; their problems will change. A preschool teacher will enjoy children for what they are. The Bible says no one can grow taller by taking thought, nor is it likely that any preschool teacher can change a two-year-old into a ten-year-old or a four-year-old into a fourteen-year-old. Teachers of young children must accept the children where they are and enjoy them and their activities.

Preschool teachers may need to be champions of a cause as yet unrecognized by the church. A walk through many of our churches would indicate that the average church is not thinking of young children. Many times the small children are placed in undesirable rooms, and the best rooms are reserved for the adults. Yes, adults do deserve good facilities, but adults can give and allocate money for better facilities. Preschoolers cannot. Then, too, most adults are attending church because they believe what the church teaches. Preschoolers, on the other hand, are in the process of deciding what to believe. If the room and its furnishings will lead young children to the Savior more quickly, let's provide that room. The young child is looking for beauty and for a feeling of being loved. Will he or she find them in your church?

A preschool teacher must be ready to reach children through being childlike. What does this mean? Walk into the typical preschool Sunday School room. Can you tell what the children would like or what would be unattractive to them? Can you see the surroundings as helping or hindering a lesson? How would you like to bend your head back and look about twelve feet up to see the picture a teacher holds? This is an exaggeration, of course, but when a tall adult stands, holding a picture under his or her chin and looking down at the little people seated below knee level, the effect is the same.

A childlike teacher can see the world through a child's eyes, think as a child, see the joy and excitement of life. Such a teacher has some understanding of the importance of play, and will try to think concretely and literally instead of using abstract thoughts and figurative or symbolic language. A childlike teacher will realize how much each child needs a teacher, and will realize the need to understand the teacher's role.

Discipline and the Ideal Teacher

The attitude of the teacher is the most important factor in the discipline of preschoolers. Discipline must develop self-control, not merely elicit behavior pleasing to the teacher. In guiding young children, you will recognize that they need a great deal of individual attention and are likely to become overstimulated when the group becomes too large or the activities too exciting. Two-year-olds enjoy being with six to eight other children, three-year-olds with about ten other preschoolers, and four- and five-year-olds should not be in groups of more than twenty to twenty-five children.

Discipline will surely include setting the example. Preschoolers need this kind of help for motivation and because they sometimes do not know what they are to do. Are you ready to pick up 54 blocks; to mend and straighten books; to clean tables; to pick up odd bits of paper and rearrange crayons and scissors; to live with children in ways that show them your love for the Lord? This is all part of the teaching-learning ministry with preschoolers.

Remember that discipline is not just for the child who flagrantly breaks the rules and squeezes you into a corner in which you must do something. Discipline and punishment should not be considered synonymous. Try to think of discipline as a means of helping children govern their own behavior in ways which are good for them and good for others.

THE HUGGABLE LEARNERS

Any limits you set should be realistic and should be for the good of the children:

"We don't let children hurt each other."

"We don't want children to take all of the blocks when other children need some to play with, too."

"We don't let people throw puzzle pieces around so they are lost. Then no one else can play with the puzzle."

"We don't let children tear books so that other children can't read them."

This type of approach is sensible to preschoolers. They can see the value of limits such as these, realizing that they too will benefit from these regulations. Such brief explanations are more effective than merely saying, "You mustn't grab all the blocks!" "You can't play with the puzzles if you throw the pieces." Set the rule that unacceptable behavior denies a child some of the materials, but be sure your explanation is brief and complete enough to help the child understand.

Do you realize that if you commend a child when he is doing well, it will be easier to redirect his future wrong actions? Teachers who zero in on a child only when he is misbehaving are not helping that child to develop as a whole person. Every child needs to like himself, to feel wanted and worthy. But if your personal comments come only when the child is misbehaving, you are doing him a disservice. The child who is told when he does something well learns to accept himself, is eager to grow and develop, and can enjoy others.

Children are constantly working with attitudes toward themselves and others, and teachers must help them. One Sunday morning, for example, four-year-old Tom made the rounds. "Do you like me?" he kept asking the other boys. He was trying to discover how others felt about him.

In setting limits, you may sometimes say, "You can't do finger painting today, but you can work with clay." When you deny some activity or object, you will find it helpful to you and the child if you suggest an alternative. Respect a child as a person so that he will come to respect himself. Be trustworthy and accept the child's need for dependence on you without making him feel "little" or inferior.

How do you treat parents in the Preschool Department? They should always be welcome visitors. You will want to recommend that they observe, however, not participate. Tell parents of new children not to sneak out of the room unobserved by their child. Imagine how you would feel if your source of security suddenly disappeared! It is much better for Mother or Father to say ahead of time, "After a while I may go to my class, but my coat (or some other object) will be here on the chair. I'll get it when I come back for you."

Do not give children more responsibility than they can handle. It is ridiculous to expect preschoolers to put all materials away on their own, for example. The same is true of sending threes and fours into the hall by themselves to get drinks from the water fountain. Young children want an adult around who knows the way and who will help them behave as they should.

Teachers Need Rules, Too

Learning to teach young children is a continuing process. You will never know all there is to know. Your first requisite is a sincere love for the Lord. Next, you should love little children. Then as you continue to study children, materials, and methods, remember the following simple rules.

1. *Put safety first.* This rule will help you consider the health and welfare of every child.

2. *Always speak to individual children by name.* Speak quietly and clearly, in positive rather than negative terms. You may say, "Bobby, we use the crayons on paper," instead of "Children, don't use the crayons on the wall." Preschoolers will respond better to personal recognition; in fact, many may not "hear" until you use their names.

3. *Speak and act as though you expect your suggestions to be carried out.* Perhaps some two-year-olds are throwing blocks. Touch the child or children lightly on arm or shoulder, saying, "Blocks are for building." Then pile a few blocks yourself, inviting the children to join you.

4. *Try to stop trouble before it starts.* When you see a two-year-old preparing to take a plaything from another child, offer a similar plaything or substitute one which might serve the purpose.

5. *Don't always offer options—or deny them.* Discriminate between situations in which a child has a choice, and ones in which routines must be carried out.

6. *Treat children with courtesy and respect.* In all your relationships be friendly, interested, and understanding.

The best teacher is a concerned human being first and always.

Teachers in a Preschool Department must develop a team attitude. With older children, the individual teacher may be the star performer, but young children need a team of teachers. Teachers should take turns in guiding the activities. Even though there may be only a half-dozen children in the department, teaching and learning will be more effective if responsibilities are shared by more than one teacher.

Teachers of young children should be regular in attendance, giving the children a feeling of security because the same adults are waiting for them each week. Regularity is in first place, but punctuality cannot be divorced from it. Teachers must come on time in order to be unhurried, to greet the first child, and to have the room and materials ready.

Primaries and juniors can, if necessary, help set up their own rooms and activities, but preschoolers cannot. Materials must be ready for preschoolers. Books must be displayed attractively, materials laid out for art activities, learning centers arranged for use, and a record player or flannel board ready and waiting. You will want children to help whenever they can, but during preschool years their interest in helping will be fleeting and their abilities limited.

Early childhood teachers recognize that they must create the environment for spiritual learning. They will be prepared to structure learning experiences, but they will also be flexible enough to change according to pupil needs and teachable moments.

"Know what? We have a new puppy," says one of your preschoolers just as you are ready to tell the Bible story. What do you do? First, if at all possible, you encourage preschoolers to talk when they first come into Sunday School. If a child interrupts in this way, however, you can make him or her feel happy by recognizing his or her contribution—*and* you can continue the story. You could say, "How happy you must be to have a new puppy!" Or, "We're glad you have a puppy, Dan!" Then continue with the Bible story. You have not asked a question which would demand more conversation. You did not ask other children how they felt and thus started many children thinking about dogs. You recognized the child's feelings, but continued with your lesson.

Do you have a happy face? A preschool teacher needs

to wear one. Good teachers lead children to learn, and to learn with joy.

Do you become excited when you realize that a young child is discovering the reality of God's love? Perhaps someone asks for prayer for his or her father or mentions a weekday experience that enables you to see spiritual truth linked to life.

Good teachers are not born but are made through their efforts and through the work of the Lord Jesus in their lives. You, teacher, can never do the Lord's work in the hearts of your pupils, but you can grow in your knowledge of the Lord, His Word, and your pupils. You can pray for each child, the stubborn and misbehaving, the unloved and perverse. You can prepare to the best of your ability and then depend on God to use you!

REACT

1. To make God real to a young child, we must surround him or her with people to whom God is real. Why is this true?

2. Jesus said, "Everyone who is fully trained will be like his teacher" (Lk. 6:40). What does this mean for you as a teacher?

ACT

1. Make a list of the qualifications given in this chapter. Give yourself a score, varying from excellent (1) to poor (5) on each qualification.

2. What is the most important step you can take now to grow in your own relationship with the Lord?

CHAPTER THREE
WHAT ARE PRESCHOOLERS LIKE?

▶Preschoolers are motion and sound! They are wigglers and questioners. They speak with their bodies as well as their tongues. They are curious, questioning, and active. Every one of them is unique from every other preschooler! Each one insists on "being me."

Preschoolers are children between the ages of two and five—little people who want to feel big. They have very special spiritual needs that you can help to meet. These needs as well as the Bible truths they can understand are discussed fully in Chapter 4; the present chapter will describe preschoolers and make some generalizations about their development.

Every preschooler can learn about God and grow in spiritual understanding. How the child grows depends on how you teach and what you understand about his or her particular characteristics. What preschoolers can learn and how you will teach are important subjects—so important that they deserve special chapters in this book. This chapter focuses on the development of preschoolers, describing certain characteristics of each year of development. Sometimes every month makes a big difference in the life of a young child.

Some things are the same about most preschoolers, but many things are not the same! Therefore, do not combine all preschoolers, two through five, in one group and expect to teach them efficiently. Preschoolers learn more in small groups: five or six in a group is best for two- and three-year-olds; and *never* more than twenty to twenty-five in a group of four- and five-year-olds.

Some preschoolers look bigger than others of the same age. When this is the case, teachers are tempted to think that "big" children should know more and be more responsible—or that the "small" preschooler is exceptional for his or her age. But all preschoolers, regardless of age, are somewhere in the process of growing from "me" to "we" as they see the example of adults and respond to their teaching. All children are interested in "becoming," wanting to feel "big," and believing that they can learn and do, just as God Himself intended.

Preschoolers have hungry senses. They want to see, touch, hear, smell, push, pull, smash, move, and taste. These young children need to move; they *cannot* be still for a long time. Adults should not try to equate being *still* with being *good,* for preschoolers are limited in the length of time they can remain quiet. Their muscles scream to move! Two-year-olds seem to need constant activity, but five-year-olds can control their need to move and be quiet as long as they are really interested. When teachers recognize preschoolers' need to move, they plan programs to alternate between quiet and active times. Active time provides for bodily movement, and quiet time is listening time.

WHAT ARE PRESCHOOLERS LIKE?

Not only do preschoolers want to move, but they also want to talk. A young child feels that his or her talking is more important than yours—and wants his turn even if you have to stop! You should always plan for a time in Sunday School when children can talk; a time early in the hour is better than halfway through the session. You may want to come early to greet individual children, or you may encourage conversation at interest centers, but you *must* plan for conversation with your preschoolers.

During the years from two to five, children make great physical progress. Large muscle coordination improves, but the small muscles do not develop as rapidly or as well. Preschoolers' physical capabilities grow from the first steps of the toddler to the running and skipping abilities of five-year-olds. Eye-hand coordination develops during these years. Some preschoolers, especially those who are four and five, may do well at pasting, cutting, threading beads, or performing other intricate work. The average preschooler, however, is happiest when he is using his large muscles to clap, stretch, run, bend, and sway.

Preschoolers are curious. They ask limitless questions! "What is it? Why?" they want to know. If you listen carefully, you'll discover that these little people are proficient in finding out why, who, where, when, how, and what. Young children often like to ask the same question over and over, as they retest their knowledge or that of adults. Questioning can also be a means of getting attention, something all children want and need.

By all means, encourage preschoolers' curiosity. Praise them for wanting to find out by providing some answers and helping them to discover other answers for themselves. Adults need to be ready to give direction but not to smother the questioner with information. Someone has said, "Don't answer questions the pupils aren't asking." The same philosophy applies to conversation with preschoolers. An older child resents long explanations when he doesn't need them and may say so, but when preschoolers lose interest, they dart off to something that does attract them.

Depending on his age, a preschooler may be quite adventuresome. Two-year-olds are content to climb for the fun and adventure of climbing, but four- and five-year-olds want to climb the slide in order to come down backward. In play skills, preschoolers move from the block-piling stage of age two to the building of intricate structures designed by fives or fours. Two-year-olds are likely to color with long movement of crayon on paper. Five-year-olds, on the other hand, will work carefully to perfect a recognizable drawing.

Remember that a young child's emotions are very near the surface. Tears may erupt because of loneliness, a lost shoe buckle, competition from another child, or failure to hang onto a favorite toy or possession. The Christian teacher must be careful not to capitalize on emotional response when telling a Bible story or reprimanding unacceptable behavior.

Now that we have described some of the general characteristics of preschoolers, let's look at each age, noting some of the recognizable differences.

Who Is Two?

We are beginning our study of preschoolers at age two, the year when children usually begin attending Sunday School. Being two is important, and both church and home need to recognize the two-year-olds who are passing from toddler stage to the runabout age. A child of two is self-aware. He or she can understand when an adult says, "Who made Ann? God made Ann."

A two-year-old may appear to be a very negative person. But the child's frequent use of *no* should not be interpreted as mere obstinacy or contrariness. A two-year-old is trying out the word *no* and sometimes means, "Don't rush me. Let me look some more. Wait till I'm ready." Ignore the *no* when possible, or invite the child to change activity. A two-year-old is just at the edge of considering other people, both children or adults. Some two-year-olds will challenge the aggressive behavior of another child, but others will look on helplessly while the aggressive child walks away with a favorite toy.

Play for most two- and three-year-olds is generally parallel play. The term *parallel play* is used to describe children who play *side by side*, either at the same activity, such as using clay or blocks, or who play at different activities, such as pounding a peg block and dressing a doll.

Two-year-olds may be ready to experiment with friendship, offering a toy to another child or responding in some other way, but they really are not ready to share. It is usually better if a teacher offers the second child a substitute toy or activity instead of insisting that the first child give up what he feels is rightfully his. Of course, a teacher may sometimes suggest, "Tommy would like a turn, too. Please let him play with your toy after a while."

A two-year-old may still be quite cuddly, or so independent that he or she does not want to be held or picked up. The child's vocabulary may be large or small. Though the child has probably learned to feed himself or herself, such delicate operations as cutting with a knife or stabbing a bite of food with a fork are usually beyond his or her ability. Recognize these limits

29

and plan handwork activities that do not tire and frustrate the child.

Two-year-olds like routine. If they are accustomed to finding things in a certain place, they can learn to put them back again. Don't hesitate to expect two-year-olds to help put toys away, but avoid making cleanup time such a chore that children become resentful and fussy. Conversation or a song helps them join you and others in putting things away. A song one nursery teacher uses is repetition of the phrase, "I'm helping, I'm helping because I love Jesus." Sometimes she varies it to say, "I'm picking up scraps (or blocks or toys) because I love Jesus."

Who Is Three?
A three-year-old is still developing large muscle control, but is sure on his or her feet. The child plays hard and tires easily. If interested, he or she pays attention—but once you have lost that interest, you have lost the child.

Three-year-olds are not too different from two-year-olds in darting from one activity to another. That is why interest centers are important in the Nursery Department. Children at age three are more flexible than they were at two; they respond to your suggestions and your plans for structured play. Still, both twos and threes are essentially very egocentric.

A child of three is less negative than the two-year-old. This is partly because he is in better command of himself and his environment; he knows his way around. Three-year-olds will play together in a limited way, but they still enjoy playing alone.

Adults will find three-year-olds more ready to talk to them and to other children because they have a larger vocabulary and feel more comfortable about nursery activities. Do not lose your opportunities for conversation. Be sure to listen as much or more than you talk. When you do have something to say, try to guide the conversation meaningfully, choosing words to help children learn. If a child comments about his or her new shoes, you might say, "They're pretty." But you could make your conversation mean more by responding, "Aren't they pretty? Wasn't it good of Daddy (or Mother) to buy them for you? Have you thanked God for your new shoes?"

A three-year-old is quite capable of bargaining for what he or she wants. A two-year-old may grab a toy, but a three-year-old will try trading it for another or inviting the other child to share by telling what he or she will do with it. Brent's suggestion to Keith illustrates this idea. Keith brought a small toy motorcycle to the Nursery Department. Brent wanted to play with it, too. Here is the conversation that gave Brent a turn.

"What's that?" asked Brent, though he knew the answer.

"My motorcycle," replied Keith.

"I could make it go fast. Want to see?" offered Brent.

Brent raced the motorcycle across the room and then carefully returned it to Keith, saying, "See how fast I did it?"

Preschoolers like to feel big by helping. Three-year-olds are usually ready to be helpers as long as an adult does not insist a job always be finished or done exactly according to adult standards. Let three-year-olds do what they can; do not kill their desire to help by requiring too much of them.

Who Is Four?
Four is a stormy age, but much less physical than two

or three. Two- and three-year-olds hit with their fists, and sometimes they kick and bite. Four- and five-year-olds are more likely to use words or actions that show disregard and disapproval.

Betty had a birthday. At Sunday School, Scott was invited to help her blow out the candles on the artificial birthday cake. But Todd rushed to the front of the room, hoping to blow out candles, too. The teacher sent Todd back to his chair. Four-year-old Todd did not cry, but when Scott sat down again, Todd tried spitting at him. Todd kept up this effort to condemn Scott by spitting and blowing till a teacher forcibly moved him to another chair.

Four-year-olds begin to be fascinated by words. They like the sound of new words. They are delighted when they make up "silly" words of their own. At four, perhaps even earlier, many children invent imaginary playmates who serve them well. On more than one occasion, Jackie described her imaginary friend, Judy, so vividly that a well-meaning but unknowing hostess sent home another portion of birthday treats "for Judy."

The four-year-old may seem big and grown up, but he is not. He still needs adult help and direction. Four-year-olds respond well to adults because they are beginning to recognize that both children and adults have feelings. Many children of four are ready to play happily with another child, often selecting a "best" friend of the same sex.

Four-year-olds are adventuresome. They enjoy trying more things by themselves—both physical and mental. Growing often means new experiences for children of this age.

Who Is Five?
Five is a comfortable age, not nearly as stormy and

boisterous as four. A child of five has good control over his body. His large muscles are much better developed, but he still has difficulty with the small muscles that control his fingers and hands. Five-year-olds should use large brushes and crayons in their art activities. They have passed the stage of merely smearing or dabbing with art materials and are working purposefully, knowing what they want to achieve. Five-year-olds will work for 20 minutes or longer at an activity that really interests them.

Five-year-olds usually know how to take turns and respect other people's belongings. According to the direction provided by adults, they are learning right from wrong and recognize in many situations what they should do. These children love stories, but they like best the stories that teach something new about places, persons, or interesting things.

Between the ages of two to six, most children gain from 500 to 600 new words a year. Therefore, the five-year-old may have a vocabulary of 3,000 words, but you must still be sure that he understands the meaning or meanings of words. Too many classic stories are told of preschoolers who misunderstood. For example, did the "pilot" who judged Jesus also fly a plane? Was Abraham's tent like the one a child's family bought from Sears? Five-year-olds are still thinking very literally and concretely. They are no more ready for symbolism than they were at three or four.

Five-year-olds are conformists, doing what they see other children or adults do. Though perhaps further along in growing unselfish, moving from the "me" to the "we" viewpoint, children of five are still very self-centered. Yet they are more aware of others and are growing in friendliness and concern. Because they can play with others and enjoy it, they will feel left out if not included in group activities. A two-year-old may wander off when he or she does not feel part of a group, but a five-year-old will stand alone and suffer the terrible pangs of loneliness and insecurity.

Five-year-olds are still physically active and rely on their senses to help them learn. Nevertheless, these preschoolers will ask more thoughtful questions and will want to talk longer and more often when they gain an adult's attention. Five-year-olds are on the brink of the wonderful world of reading books. They are almost ready to stop being preschoolers and to become "big" first graders.

Do not be tricked by this artificial division made by some adults. Six-year-olds still enjoy make-believe and running and shouting. They do not suddenly become quiet and lose their love and need of physical activity. No, six is just the next year when children still grow in feeling big and independent. Six-year-olds are different in some ways from five-year-olds, but do not expect that when a five-year-old leaves your Sunday School department he or she will change overnight into a really big boy or girl. If you have been watching individuals and trying to "learn" your children, you have seen your five-year-olds becoming more and more like six throughout the year.

Do You Really Know?
Now you have some general ideas about children during their preschool years. But do you know each child individually? Can you honestly say you are aware of individual feelings? When have you been interested enough to really listen? Who among your groups is shy and needs to be drawn out of his or her timidity?

How well do you know the homes of your children? Whose grandfather is sick? Who vacations in a camper or tent? What children compete for attention with older brothers and sisters? Who is an only child and may not identify when you talk about brothers and sisters? What child in your group feels displaced because a new baby requires all of Mother's attention?

It is not enough to know generalities. Use the characteristics given in this book as a good beginning to help you concentrate on knowing each child. Take time to listen to your children, because through listening you will discover needs. Then you will begin to see your children as distinct individuals. You will pray more specifically and prepare with enthusiasm because you know Johnny, Jenny, Sam, and all the others.

REACT

1. What is the single most important characteristic of preschoolers? Do you agree it is their need to move and develop through their senses?

2. Think of a preschooler you know. Can you see the "me" stage in his or her attitudes? When do you see the child's awareness of "we"?

ACT

1. If you are teaching preschoolers, what activities do you provide to take care of the need to move?

2. What kinds of activities seem likely to promote learning for preschoolers?

CHAPTER FOUR
WHAT CAN THEY LEARN?

▶ "From infancy you have known the holy Scriptures, which are able to make you wise for salvation through faith in Christ Jesus" (II Tim. 3:15).

"Can a little child really learn about God?" asks someone who has never worked with little children. The questioner has never read a book on early childhood development and does not understand the capacities of little children. He tends to excuse the lack of spiritual objectives in a program for young children.

Experience, the Word of God, and young children themselves all testify to the value of early instruction in spiritual truth. Young children can learn to know God, to love Jesus, to respect the Bible, and to grow in love toward others. It is during the early years that lifelong attitudes are formed. These are foundational years; the foundation must be carefully built so that it will not be necessary to remove any inferior material from the foundation later. Spiritual truth learned at two, three, four, and five should be held true for life.

Some religious educators have drawn the conclusion that our younger children actually cannot learn concepts that will be "true for life." The research of

WHAT CAN THEY LEARN?

Swiss psychologist Jean Piaget and others has shown
that children's minds are simply unable to grasp many
abstract or complicated ideas. There will always be
some distortion in a child's thinking.

Just ask a preschooler how old he or she thinks you
are, and you may get an interesting answer. One may
think you are very, very old—"Seventeen, maybe?" Or
take a trip with a child. One of the first questions he or
she may ask is, "How far is it?" And even if you say,
"It's 120 miles to Grandpa's house," ten minutes into
your journey you're likely to hear a little voice asking,
"Are we there yet?" Age and distance are both very
hard for young children to grasp, even though they
know the words "old" and "miles." So, the argument
goes, isn't it much more difficult for boys and girls to
grasp the meaning of "God" and to understand Bible
truths?

Using reasoning like this, some religious educators
have argued that necessary distortions in children's
religious concepts mean that later they must "unlearn"
ideas taught in early childhood. Wouldn't it be better,
these educators ask, if we waited to teach boys and girls
about God until they were old enough to *really*
understand Biblical teachings and concepts?

This argument is, of course, based on a fallacy. Young
boys' and girls' concepts of age and distance are
distorted—but how foolish it would be if we never
mentioned these concepts until children could measure
years and miles accurately! How foolish it would be if
we never mentioned numbers until a child was old
enough to multiply and divide fractions!

The fact is that basic concepts *must* be introduced in
early childhood. As a child grows, he or she will come
to understand better and better what is involved in
"age" and "numbers." But the basic concepts must be

present for any development to take place!

In the same way, we *must* introduce young children to the concepts of God, of prayer, of the Bible, and other basic truths. Yes, their understanding will grow and change over the years. But unless those concepts are rooted in the child's thinking in the first place, he or she will grow up with a view of the world and of life in which God has no place at all!

Every concept a young child has develops and changes over time. To some extent such change always involves "unlearning." Children discard the idea that they can travel 120 miles in ten minutes, just as they discard the idea that God lives upstairs in their houses. But how important it is that as they grow, children know God exists, that He cares. With this basic knowledge deeply rooted in their personalities, they can and will grow. The ministry of planting, of impressing these most basic and foundational concepts of our faith, is the ministry of preschool teachers.

Because spiritual training in early years is important, you must clarify your objectives and be sure these goals are reached through clear and careful teaching. To set goals, you must understand the children, because you cannot teach them what they are not ready to receive.

Another Look at Nursery Children

Remember that nursery children believe most of what they hear. Through what they hear in Sunday School, their hunger for God can be encouraged and fed. The nursery child cannot understand symbolism, so teach simply, using words that mean what the child understands them to say. Preschool Departments are not the places to talk about Jesus as the Vine, the Captain, the Master, or the Door. Let two- and three-year-olds know that Jesus is the Son of God and their best Friend.

Young children have a very short attention span. They will not listen to a Bible story for more than three to five minutes. They will learn through asking questions, so allow ample opportunity for pupils to talk at any time throughout your session.

Your example will mean more than almost anything else in the nursery department because these children almost literally "catch" religion from you. How do you handle the Bible? How does your voice sound when you talk about the Lord or pray to Him? How do you show your love for the children?

Another Look at Fours and Fives

A kindergartner's feelings are very near the surface, with fear as the most outstanding emotion. How much this child needs to know the Lord as his living, loving Friend and think about God in a very personal way. Four- and five-year-olds also believe what they hear. If Bible stories are chosen to meet their needs, they will believe and apply the spiritual truth being taught.

In working with preschoolers, move at their pace, planning well so that you do not abruptly ask them to interrupt their activities in order to meet your schedules. Preschoolers are unaware of time and need a quiet atmosphere to think well. They need praise, though not overdone, for right actions. No teacher should use fear as punishment, a rather common method for many parents who say, "The policeman (that lady, store clerk) will take you away if you don't behave." Certain Bible stories that may provoke fear should be left untold till children are older.

Your own example will teach a child quietly and consistently at every age. Be sure that what your children observe backs up what you say!

The teacher of preschoolers is responsible for his or her own strong, personal foundation in Bible truth, based on Scripture. No individual or single department can carry the total responsibility; every teacher must do his or her part to know the Word of God and learn how to share it with preschoolers. You must not let the pressure of time force you to concentrate so intently on what you want to accomplish that you lose sight of individual needs.

Children learn spiritual values at church, at home, and as they mingle with others who express their faith in a variety of ways. You must recognize that you cannot regulate times for learning spiritual truths as you may some skills, such as learning to work a zipper, fasten a button, or tie a shoe. Attitudes and feelings can never be taught with this approach. That is why every children's worker needs to be aware of teachable moments, sensing the leading of the Holy Spirit. Singing a song, saying a verse, or praying is not worship unless the child's attitude is directed Godward.

How, then, can you teach spiritual truths and lead children to love God and worship Him? First, through your own example. Next, plan for the child to encounter and understand spiritual truth. Watch for reactions and relationships. Is there an unhappy or happy time when a child's thoughts can be directed to God? Any happy experience a preschooler has had may be an occasion to thank the Lord. A family or a personal problem expressed by a child may be a prayer request.

Skill in guiding conversation is not learned overnight! To guide children to spiritual truth requires prayer, an openness and awareness of the Holy Spirit's leading, and experience with children. Many teachers who pray much about their teaching find themselves saying

words and expressing ideas that have come to them
only from the Holy Spirit. They admit that the ideas
have not been part of their lesson preparation, but have
been brought to mind as they talked with pupils and
sensed their needs. The Holy Spirit is a wonderful
Partner and Guide in our teaching!

Later chapters will deal with methods; this chapter
will examine what a young child can learn. Cramming
Bible facts into children's heads does not guarantee that
Bible truths will be understood and assimilated. Unless
you have goals and objectives for a Bible-based learning
program, you may accomplish very little in helping
children. Goals make the difference!

What can be accomplished in preschool years? The
following goals have been compiled on the basis of age-
group objectives as set up by both denominational and
independent publishers of Sunday School literature.

What Twos and Threes Can Learn
Even young children are ready for many of the basic
truths of Scripture if these truths are presented at their
own level.

Twos and threes can learn about God:
▶ They understand that God loves them.
▶ They begin to show an attitude of trust in God and
dependence on Him.
▶ They understand that God is with them in all
places.
▶ They know God will hear when they talk to Him.
▶ They recognize that God made all things.

Twos and threes can learn about Jesus Christ:
▶ They can understand that God sent Jesus.

▶ They realize that Jesus loves children and wants them to love Him.
▶ They know that Jesus can do hard things that no one else can do.
▶ They grow in their realization that Jesus was a special baby.
▶ They know that Jesus can see and hear them.
▶ They can understand that Jesus died, came back to life, and now lives in Heaven.

On the basis of this knowledge, children grow in love for the Lord Jesus and their desire to please Him.

Twos and threes can learn about the Bible:
▶ They know the Bible is God's Book, a very special Book.
▶ They want to hear God's Word and do what God says in His Book.
▶ They understand selected Bible stories and associate the Bible with feelings of love, reverence, and respect for God.

Twos and threes can learn about their own attitudes:
▶ They will pray simple, familiar prayers of petition and thanksgiving.
▶ They can give their money to God's house.
▶ They will grow in their desire to please God by obeying.
▶ They are glad that Jesus loves them and are thankful for His daily care.

What Fours and Fives Can Learn
Here the need is not for heavy doctrine but for the comfort of His presence, His love and His care.

Fours and fives can learn about God:
- ▶ They build on their growing knowledge of God to understand that God's love includes themselves and others.
- ▶ They realize they can pray to God at any time and place.
- ▶ They know God is the Creator and loving Heavenly Father.
- ▶ They begin to understand that God is the Sustainer of all things and provides them with the necessities of life. They are growing in their awareness that God cares for them through their parents and others.
- ▶ They begin to feel a personal responsibility to God as the One they should love and want to obey. They are grateful to God for His provision and love.
- ▶ They are beginning to understand that God sent Jesus to die for everyone's sin, including their own.
- ▶ They know that sin is disobedience to God, and that God will forgive sin when they are genuinely sorry and ask for forgiveness.

Fours and fives can learn about Jesus Christ:
Adding to the spiritual foundation laid in earlier years, children of this age know that Jesus is God's Son and is their best Friend who loves them. They realize that Jesus is living now after dying for everyone's sin.
- ▶ They realize that Jesus will help them obey (share, help).
- ▶ They know Jesus has the same power God has.
- ▶ They are learning to pray in the name of Jesus.

Fours and fives can learn about the Bible:
- ▶ They know the Bible is a special Book and contains wonderful stories of Jesus.

THE HUGGABLE LEARNERS

▶ They realize that God's Word tells them what to do.
▶ They are growing in their ability to distinguish Bible stories as real, unlike other stories of imagination and fancy.

Fours and fives can learn about their own attitudes and actions:

▶ They are learning to pray at any time, in any place, and for everyone.
▶ They can praise God by giving thanks.
▶ They are growing in their concern for others, missions, church, and other children.
▶ They are growing in their love for God and Jesus, wanting to obey God, parents, and teachers.
▶ They are ready to show often that they can share, be kind, and tell others about Jesus.
▶ They have a growing feeling of trust and security in God's love.
▶ They want to hear Bible stories, sometimes recalling favorites.
▶ They can sometimes help explain how they should act on the basis of the spiritual truth taught in a story.

Belief and Behavior

Children who love the Lord will change their behavior. A five-year-old was the despair of a local storekeeper. Every time this child came into his store, she played with displays until something was broken or the display toppled to the floor. Unfortunately, her parents did not see their responsibility in changing her conduct. One August day, however, the little girl came into the store, and the storekeeper, although not glad to see the child, realized he had not seen her for several months. She stayed with her mother and did more looking than touching. She responded to questions with polite answers. At last the storekeeper could stand it no longer. Rather bluntly he said, "Your daughter seems to have changed a lot this summer." Her mother, not a Christian, said, "Yes, we've noticed it, too. I think it's because she went to Vacation Bible School this summer."

After a child becomes a Christian—and some children do even as preschoolers—you may notice some behavioral changes, but you cannot expect perfection from these young children any more than you would from an adult. The preschooler will grow in dependence on the Lord, in frequent use of prayer, and in the desire to love the Lord and obey Him. The child is a new creature in Christ, but he or she is still a child.

Teachers must be careful not to define as sin what is normal behavior for a preschooler. No teacher should ever try to control behavior by saying, "If you love Jesus, you will . . ." Assume that a child does love Jesus. Say, "Because we love Jesus, we want to take turns." Remember that Christian behavior is motivated by love for the Lord. Do not use a negative, corrective approach, implying that one who loves God will never have a wrong attitude or perform a wrong action.

Having learned what children can grasp concerning God, Jesus, the Bible, and attitudes, you must also realize that head knowledge is not enough. As you teach spiritual truth, you will want to watch for feelings or attitudes and actions. Some actions and attitudes are listed in a curriculum's age-group objectives. Evaluate your teaching by the feelings and actions you are able to observe, realizing that many attitudes will be exhibited at home.

Perhaps parents will share with you moments when their children expressed thankfulness to the Lord, love for Jesus, and a growing dependence on God. Parents may be the ones to notice the prayer lives of their children, the Sunday School songs they sing, and the frequency with which they ask for a Bible story. A mother may be the one to report that her child asks every day, "Is today the day we go to church?" More than a few teachers have been overjoyed to find that Sunday School is a very important event in the lives of their preschoolers.

How do you reach these goals and objectives? You do so week by week through finger plays, stories, music, prayer, moments of worship, creative activities, and visual aids—all presented after prayerful preparation. Every week, children should leave your department with new information—but also with a clear understanding of a specific way in which they can demonstrate their love for and obedience to the Lord. Preschool teachers must have long-range goals, as exemplified in a curriculum's age-group objectives, and short-range goals, as identified in weekly or unit teaching aims.

Teachers in the preschool departments need to understand the limitations of little children, even as they realize the importance of laying spiritual foundations. After a Primary Department teacher presents the story of Jesus and faithfully exhibits love for Him, he or she may have the joy of seeing an actual decision for Christ. But training in the preschool years has an important place in the child's finding the Lord as Savior and in growing into the fullness of the Christian life.

Conversion and Preschoolers
Usually when adults talk about helping a child "know Jesus," their focus is on conversion. So it's important to

ask whether or not our youngest children can come to know Jesus in this sense.

Certainly there is a time when each person must make a personal decision concerning Jesus Christ—a time when one realizes that he or she is invited to become God's child in a very special sense.

Ultimately our efforts to help our children know Jesus are meant to include their making this choice, and going on to grow in this exciting personal relationship. But it's hard to say just when an individual is ready to make a commitment to Christ. It's not necessary for us as teachers to try to solve the difficult theological question of how old a boy or girl must be to experience conversion. Instead we are to guide our boys and girls to know Jesus in an increasingly meaningful way, as preparation for conversion if not through conversion itself. When we provide a context for a continuous, growing appreciation of Jesus, we make our most significant contribution to children's lives.

Conversion is a Christian doctrine, and a vital one. The conversion experience is central to our faith. But growth in appreciating Jesus is the central issue of our ministry to the youngest. I personally believe preschoolers can experience conversion, and am sure my own children experienced conversion at early ages. But conversion did not come because I constantly emphasized the Gospel message. It came because in home and church we tried to help young Paul and Timothy and Joy sense Jesus as a real Person who loved them—and who, like Mom and Dad, was ready to forgive them when they did wrong.

How will you deal with a young child who wants to receive Jesus as Savior? Talk to the child alone. Explain that although God loves everyone, He cannot have sin (or badness) in Heaven. Jesus came and took the punishment for our badness. He died on the cross so that God can forgive our sin. When we tell Him we are sorry we have sinned, God forgives us and takes away our sin.

How does the young child define his or her sin? This will be some indication to you of the child's understanding. Does he or she want to talk to God about it? If not, do not force the issue. The child is evidently feeling a need, but may not be ready to receive Christ as Savior. If the child does want to talk to God about his or her sin, encourage the child to repeat a prayer after you. It could be something like, "Dear Lord, I know I have done wrong. I am sorry for my sin. I want You to be my Savior and forgive me. In Jesus' name. Amen."

Churches should choose a Sunday School curriculum that is Bible-based and evangelical, written by trained Christian educators who may even have pretested the lessons. These experienced teachers will help you to lead young children to grow spiritually, preparing them for the day when they will understand their need of a Savior.

REACT
A compilation of letters written by children to God has furnished many adults with some good laughs. What would you do if you heard one of your preschoolers say, "God is an old man with many eyes"? How about "God lives at church and then goes back to Heaven. That's all He sees"? Or, "God is like a policeman. He don't want you to do nothing"?

ACT
1. Telling children about God is not enough. You must

try to lead them to think about Him and trust Him.
How can you help children make a connection
between their experiences and God? Think of one
idea or experience a child has shared with you. Were
you successful in directing the child's thoughts to
God in this incident?

2. What are your earliest memories of awareness of
   God? How have they affected your adult attitudes?

CHAPTER FIVE
THE TEACHABLE MOMENT

▶Is your teaching stuffed with facts, or is it full of ideas? Are you interested in pouring what you know into young minds and having it set like concrete, or are you concerned with helping children think and discover? One secret of good teaching is to know the pupil and respect him.

One of the most important things to understand about teaching preschoolers is the way the class hour needs to be structured. Older children are taught in a much more structured setting. Often curricula suggest 20 minutes for older children in departmentalized worship, 20 minutes with a Bible story, and 20 minutes in a workbook activity. Yet it would be disastrous to try to impose this kind of structure on preschoolers.

The reason is rooted in their characteristics. Young children have a short attention span. They can't concentrate on a single project for even ten minutes. Young children have a built-in wiggle. They have a real, physical need for movement. Sitting still for longer periods simply isn't possible for many boys and girls.

Young children also need individual attention. It's hard for many preschoolers to pay attention while seated in a group. Younger preschoolers especially are likely to feel that a teacher who is talking with a group is not talking to them. They need an adult who looks directly at them, who speaks directly to them, and they often need to listen in groups that aren't much larger than three or four persons.

It's clear, then, that programs for preschoolers must have unique structure if those programs are to effectively reach and teach our youngest boys and girls. There will be a Bible time. But it may not last for more than five or ten minutes, and even then it must often rely on visual aids and good storytelling techniques. There will be a worship time. But this, too, will be brief, expanding slightly as preschoolers pass from the threes to the fours and on to the fives.

What Makes a Good Preschool Curriculum?

What, then, are some of the elements built into typical Sunday School programs for preschoolers, and how do they work?

A good curriculum for preschoolers will have activities that the particular age—two, three, four, or five—can understand and perform. For example, it would be ridiculous to expect two-year-olds to skip to music or to work together in writing a song. Five-year-olds will be able to skip and to help write music, but they would be bored with the picture books and the simple stories two-year-olds can understand. Curriculum writers have studied children and know the materials and methods best suited to each age.

A good curriculum is planned to make every moment count. One main aim for each lesson is another good criterion for a curriculum.

51

THE HUGGABLE LEARNERS

The aims for a unit should not only include knowledge goals—what a child should know—but must also recognize that a child needs to respond through his feelings. It is not enough to tell young children the story of Jesus stilling the storm; you also want them to feel more love for and confidence in the Lord Jesus.

Another key to a good morning's session is flexibility. If the moment seems to demand music, a finger play, or a relaxing activity, the prepared teacher is ready. Sessions for two- and three-year-olds cannot be run on a rigid schedule. There will be Sundays when four and five-year-olds do not respond in the way you hoped they would. Be flexible! Remember, *you are teaching children, not lessons.* If you are constantly urging the children on to another activity because you have planned a full morning, you are really building up tension. These little people have no sense of time; that is why so many preschoolers dawdle.

It is impossible, in a book dealing with children ages two through five, to describe a specific program for you to use. But here is what a typical program for three-year-olds *could* look like:

Individual or small-
group activities — 25 minutes
Group stories — 10 minutes
Group activities — 20 minutes
Closing time — 5 minutes

A program for two-year-olds may look like the following, because they need many more individual and small group activities:

Individual activities — 40 minutes
Group stories and
activities — 10 minutes

We must recognize that not all two- and three-year-olds will join in group activities. Do not insist that they do, but frequently invite them to join. Be sure the group activities are so attractive that children will want to participate.

In the department for four- and five-year-olds, a typical program may look like this:

Individual and small-
group activities — 10 minutes
Group stories and
activities — 25 to 30 minutes
Small-group activities — 10 to 15 minutes

Follow the pattern suggested in your curriculum. You may want to make changes, but first understand what the curriculum writer is trying to accomplish. Be sure the children have plenty of opportunity to participate, because preschoolers cannot sit quietly to hear an adult talk, talk, *talk!* If you pride yourself on having a "quiet" group of four- and five-year-olds who sit around a table listening to your story and then quietly coloring some handwork, you are guilty of stifling the children and omitting some of the best learning techniques available. "Quiet children" is not the mark of the most effective learning. Perhaps the difference lies in the teacher's viewpoint. Are you proud of what *you* have *taught*, or are you happy for what the *children* have *learned*?

What is the scene in your room when the first child appears? How do you greet the children and help them enter into the day's activities? In some preschool departments, a child gives his offering when he enters. Preschoolers usually arrive individually, not in a group, and are ready for individual activities. These individual or small-group activities are described in Chapter 7.

For two-year-olds, individual activity time or interest-center learning may take the greater part of the hour. The two teaching-learning methods discussed in Chapter 6, play and guided conversation, will probably be used throughout the Sunday School hour, but they are always used in the individual or small-group activities.

Now let's turn our attention to the specific activities and teaching of the large-group time. Some lesson plans call the large-group time "circle time," "story time," "together time," or "sharing time." Regardless of the title, teachers plan this part of the session. The large-group time will include the Bible story, music, Bible verse, perhaps applicational or conduct story, prayer, playing out the story or roleplaying, and often special moments of fellowship to recognize visitors or celebrate a birthday.

The younger the child, the smaller the group. Two- and three-year-olds will do best when they are with no more than ten other children. These young children may seem to enjoy an exciting, stimulating hour, but afterward, they may be exhausted.

What About Music?
You will use music in both the large-group and the small-group or individual activities. The same criteria apply wherever music is used: *Music must be more than rhythm; the words must mean something to the young child.* One song that meets the standard for music and words is "God Made Everything," sung to the tune of "Twinkle, Twinkle, Little Star":

God made trees that grow so tall,
And the little ants very small.
Apples red, the big, bright sun,

Stars that shine when day is done.
Mommies, daddies, babies, too.
God made me, and God made you.
(From *100 Action Songs for Preschoolers,*
© 1987 by David C. Cook Publishing Co.)

All preschoolers enjoy music, but four- and five-year-olds are most likely to join you in singing. Two- and three-year-olds will listen to you, but few of them will sing with you. Listening to music is an experience all young children enjoy. The ways of listening and the necessary equipment will be discussed in Chapter 8.

What is good music for preschoolers? First, the words must say something to them. This means that the words will be within the vocabulary of the children, and the ideas in any song will be simple and few. Examine some hymns, and you will discover that there may be as many as eight ideas in one stanza. Younger preschoolers need one simple thought, as in this example from *100 Action Songs for Preschoolers* (sung to the tune of "The Farmer in the Dell"):

God takes care of me.
God takes care of me.
God takes care of everything,
And God takes care of me.

Such a simple song is well suited to two- and three-year-olds. Four- and five-year-olds, meanwhile, could handle the following number, also from *100 Action Songs for Preschoolers* (sung to the tune of "Twinkle, Twinkle, Little Star"):

I look in the Bible to see
Just what God is saying to me.

THE HUGGABLE LEARNERS

Worship God and always obey;
Talk to Jesus every day;
I look in the Bible to see
Just what God is saying to me.

Children need to learn new songs to accept the new and expanding ideas being taught. They need to sing songs to learn spiritual truths and to make these truths part of their thinking and feeling.

If you and your children sing one song after another without really knowing why, you may have a "song time"—but not a learning or thinking time. If your children sing in this way, they never really concentrate on the meaning of the words or sing with understanding.

Before teaching a song to children in a group situation, make sure they have heard the song several times. How? The pianist may use the song as quiet music; perhaps you could sing the song yourself at a strategic moment, or you may use the words of the song in guided conversation. Not until a child has really heard the message of a song can he begin to learn the song for himself. This is especially important for three-, four-, and five-year-olds. If the children hear the song several times as adults sing it, they will learn it naturally and correctly.

How many songs should you use? Another criterion for a good curriculum is the number of meaningful songs that are introduced to help children discover and review Bible truth. If you can make up simple tunes for the Bible memory verses, the verses will become more meaningful to your children. You will not want to use more songs than your children can enjoy, yet you must not repeat favorite songs endlessly. Remember, a song is a good way to introduce a new concept.

56

A word of caution about symbolism belongs in a discussion of music for young children. Remember that preschoolers, two through five, are thinking concretely and literally. Songs such as "I Am the Door," "Fishers of Men," "Give Me Oil in My Lamp," "This Little Light of Mine," and others which are figurative should be ruled out on that basis. What child wants oil from a can or bottle squirted over the lamp in the family room? How can Jesus be a door? Wait until the children are nine or older before introducing songs with symbolic language.

How Will You Use Prayer?
Prayer is important at any time! The brief sentence prayer at the interest center is just as important and sometimes more meaningful to the child than prayer in the large group. Even two- and three-year-olds may offer to pray. Their prayers may be incoherent or far removed from the topic at hand, but if the prayer is their sincere expression, be sure to welcome their voluntary contributions.

Preschoolers pray very realistically. Accept their prayers without suggesting different words or other "improvements." "Help Mommy cook good." "Help Daddy fix my doll." "Be with my daddy on the plane." Feeling must precede praying. You cannot expect a child who feels nothing for God to be willing to talk to Him. But you can expect a child who feels strongly for someone or about something to want to pray about it.

When you lead in prayer, your prayers must be short and meaningful. Give one idea at a time, in one sentence at a time! And limit your ideas! Sometimes you will want to use a prayer poem. At another time you may want to use a Bible verse to introduce prayer.

THE HUGGABLE LEARNERS

You may say, "We love You, Jesus, because You first loved us. Thank You for—"

While folded hands, closed eyes, and bowed heads help children to concentrate attention on the prayer and its purpose, you need not insist on this posture in small-group or individual activities. Help your children to realize that they can pray standing, kneeling, walking, sitting, lying down, or in any posture at any place or time.

Preschoolers can be taught to *thank* God. Two- and three-year-olds may ask God for things *(petition)* or they may continually pray, "God bless . . ." Four- and five-year-olds, however, can learn about *confession* for wrongdoing—being sorry for sin. Some kindergartners may be able to pray simple prayers of *adoration*. Many preschoolers will *intercede* for others as they pray for the needs of missionaries, families, and friends.

Help children grow in their prayer lives by using these forms of prayer: petition, thanksgiving, intercession, adoration, and confession. Part of your job is to enlarge a child's prayer life. One teacher did it this way. Five-year-old Brent continually prayed only for himself and his family. One day the teacher said to him, "Brent, do you know anyone else who needs God's help?" Brent did. He only needed the suggestion from his teacher to become a real intercessor for others.

Bible Verses and Preschoolers
Do you want a child merely to say a verse or to know what that verse means for him or her? Your answer to this question helps you select Bible verses. Children can be taught long, involved verses. They can learn by rote. But if Bible memory verses are to speak to the child, they must say something the child can live by. Check the verses in your curriculum.

Remember that God has said, "Do not merely listen to the word, and so deceive yourselves. Do what it says" (Jas. 1:22). Isn't it true that hearing or memorizing without doing should be avoided? The Bible verses in your curriculum should be used frequently in guided conversation, as an introduction to prayer or to a song, and certainly whenever they relate to an activity.

Why Tell Stories?
Just telling a story is not enough. You should tell stories to teach. The Lord Jesus told many stories to help His listeners learn. The Lost Coin, the Lost Sheep, and the Lost Son in Luke 15 are examples of His stories.

We tell stories because young children cannot absorb Bible truth unless it is in a setting that is meaningful to them. Stories provide the setting and the action that preschoolers need. The children's experiences are too limited and their way of thinking too literal to allow them to understand some of the deep truths of Scripture. Paul wrote, "All Scripture is God-breathed and is useful for teaching, rebuking, correcting and training in righteousness" (II Tim. 3:16). No little child can grasp what Paul wrote to Timothy, but a child can understand the reality of the Bible through the story of Josiah hearing the Scripture read and his response to it. Josiah's is only one of several Bible stories related to love for God's Word.

Bible stories illustrate truths we want children to have about the Lord and what He wants them to be. Stories are one of the most effective teaching methods for preschoolers. The stories we tell must be true to the Bible, because the Word of God is the only authentic external source of God's direction to us. The story must be told accurately, because we do not want children to retain "facts" which they must unlearn at a future time.

Curriculum writers choose stories that teach Bible truth and are understandable to young children. A story for two-year-olds will be little more than twenty-five to thirty sentences—all short. Four- and five-year-olds will have longer stories. Sometimes a Bible story in the curriculum will omit some facts, or the writer may have added information that is not in the Bible passage. Is this wrong? It is if the facts omitted or the information added actually change the story. There are times, however, when additional ideas make the story more understandable and really are things that could have happened.

For example, the Bible does not expressly state that the nets used by Jesus' fishermen friends went *splash* in the water. Yet you would be justified in adding such a detail to the story. Adults bring backgrounds of experience and information to the Bible facts; a young child does not have this experience which could fill in the setting, feelings, sights, and sounds. To make the story real to inexperienced children, it is justifiable to suggest some setting, as long as that setting is compatible with the known Bible facts. Nets do make a swishing sound, donkeys do walk with a clopping sound, and children in Bible days ran and shouted even as children do today. Still, additions to a Bible story, whether added by the teller or writer, must always conform to true Biblical customs, history, and geography. The added facts must be probable in the circumstances of the narrative.

Sometimes a writer omits details that would detract from the main teaching of the story or that would cause undue emotional response from little children. For example, there are several stories that could be told in a way that would emphasize fear: the robbers on the

Jericho road, the thundering armies of Egyptians who drowned, even Jacob's lonely trip. Because little children easily become emotionally involved, curriculum writers have told the stories in language children can understand and have included only the events that help accomplish the lesson aim.

Curriculum writers also suggest ways of preparing children for the unfamiliar. If a lamp, Oriental house, net, shepherd, or other Biblical object or custom is vital to the story, the writer will show you how to acquaint the children with this information in an interest center or through an individual activity.

Preschoolers are interested in the action of the story. They are not too concerned with the where and when. Skip difficult names, talking about Moses' mother, Hannah's husband, and the wicked king (Jehoiakim), for example. Emphasize the action words and conversation, omitting long descriptions. Avoid asking rhetorical questions in the story, because they will halt the flow of events and invite the children to interrupt. If you do use questions, the children will answer, and you may have difficulty getting back to the story. Do not correct yourself if some detail slips your mind. If it is important, look for an opportunity to weave it into the story later.

Do hold your Bible or have it near at hand when you tell a story. Sometimes show older preschoolers where the story appears in the Bible. Never read the Bible story from your teaching manual! Notice how a good curriculum applies the story without moralizing but by coming to a conclusion that helps a child grasp the reality of the Biblical event.

Teachers have more trouble in starting stories than they do with any other part of the story. Never start by saying, "Once upon a time," or "Long, long ago . . ."

These phrases make the story seem unreal. A good curriculum will show you how to begin a story, giving the children a reason for listening. This approach does not give away the story. An approach that tells more than it should might be, "Today we'll hear about a baby who was hidden in a basket so that a wicked king could not find him." Take a second look. How many ideas appear in that one sentence? Too many for preschoolers. Here is an approach that suggests a reason for listening. "Let's find out how a big sister took care of her baby brother."

After the story, you will want to use an appropriate follow-up activity. One of the best ways to help children feel the story is to play it. Your children will find it easy to imagine the setting. Four- and five-year-olds will have no difficulty with this type of story play, and three-year-olds will enjoy doing what they can.

For example, after the baby Moses story let the children pretend to be Miriam. They may enjoy being the mother and placing a pretend baby and his bed in a pretend river. It will not bother preschoolers for everyone to take the part of the main character. If the children suggest taking turns at playing the main character, however, recognize their request and play the story this way. Your children will not want to play all the events of the stories—just the action parts and the climax.

Rather than asking a child to play the part of the Lord Jesus, you may wish to have a teacher read or repeat the words Jesus said. For example, all of the children will enjoy lying on the floor or drooping in their chairs as you tell of the nobleman's sick son. Then when the teacher says, "Jesus made the little boy well," your children will love jumping to their feet, feeling well and strong again.

Sometimes a finger play will help children review the story and be a part of it. Always "overlearn" a finger play so that you can give it as a spontaneous, joyous experience. Do not expect preschoolers to learn the words of a finger play; you say it and demonstrate the motions. Your children will enjoy watching, some will repeat it with you, and most of them will do the motions.

After hearing and playing the story, your children are ready for the type of activities suggested in the next chapter.

REACT

1. Did you expect this chapter to include a section on worship? Why do you think it was omitted?

2. If children are to love the Bible, they must be led to think of it as a special Book that tells about God and Jesus. Do the activities described in this chapter help a child feel that way about the Bible?

ACT

1. How many times can worship take place during a Sunday School hour? We define worship as a time when a child is aware of God, of who He is, and is responding appropriately to Him. Does worship take place in your Sunday School? When? Observe to see if worship is a frequent experience. It should be.

2. How do you help your children remember the story and "feel" it?

CHAPTER SIX
PLAY AND TALK TEACHING

▶"Everything in its time" is a good slogan for preschool teachers. The time for play and guided conversation is in preschool years. The young child learns through play. He is discovering many things through the active use of his five senses. Use both play and conversation to help him understand and accept spiritual truth.

The next two chapters deal with traditional teaching methods that most Sunday School teachers recognize. This chapter helps you understand how important play and guided conversation are in the learning experience of young children. Play is more helpful to a child than any other way of learning. It is not only a way of learning, it is a way of life for the young child. Through play, the young child will learn in a short time what no one could teach him in many years.

Play As Education
Because it is hard for adults to accept the concept of play as education, let's look at how adults play and how young children play. Adults play as a change from their daily routines. Usually play costs the adult something in

time, training, or performance—golf fees, tennis court rental, or pool admissions, for example. An adult plays to relax, to escape the workday world.

What do adults learn from play? Hopefully, they learn new skills. But when adults play, enjoyment has priority. If adults labor too hard at learning to play chess or to become proficient at scuba diving, they decide it is work and may withdraw from the activity. Most adults expect to exert less mental effort in recreation than they do on the job.

Children do not take this attitude. Play is their work! Through play, they learn more than they can in any other way. They learn how to balance on a bike. They learn how to deal with others at the housekeeping center. Painting teaches them about color, while sandbox and water play introduce them to texture, structure, measurement, and perhaps new words. Through play, young children gain information, find emotional expression, understand social situations, and are freed for motor activity—their muscles move.

Your concern as a teacher is with the *content* of play and *how to use play as a teaching method!* Christian education is not primarily concerned with "free play" of a child's own choosing. While helpful to the child, free play may not move him in the direction of your goals and objectives. Christian education is concerned with educational or structured play—play with a purpose. Of course, we include some free play in our programs, but we are dealing with important spiritual truths. We plan play with a purpose.

Play as an educational device has historical support. From Froebel to Piaget, play is recognized as a means of helping a child mature. Dr. Bernard Spodek, Professor of Early Childhood Education, University of Illinois, says,

Traditionally, the field of early childhood education has been characterized by its support of play as an educational tool. Teachers at the nursery and kindergarten level organize their classrooms for play activities in the belief that through these activities young children can best learn what they are expected to learn. Even in the primary grades where direct verbal instruction is a more acceptable mode of instruction, play is still considered to be an important educative device and many of the instruction activities are developed in the form of learning games (Bernard Spodek, Teaching in the Early Years, *Englewood Cliffs, N.J.: Prentice-Hall, 1972, p. 199).*

Remember that for a play situation to be educationally useful, you must guide and supervise. It is not enough for a Christian teacher to agree that play is a good means of teaching and learning; you must also know what type of play helps learning. Unless you can begin to think of play as a learning technique, you may always feel guilty over letting children play when they "should" be seated in chairs and learning by rote.

The play pattern of young children is not stupid, silly, or a waste of time. God has planned for children to grow through playing. When a young child learns to climb a slide, put a puzzle together, or catch a ball, he is learning through play.

Jesus Christ recognized play as part of childhood, for He planned child development. He knew that when children played roles taken from the adult world, they would be getting acquainted with life. He recognized children's desire to take adult roles when, in reference to their pretend games, He said, "They are like children sitting in the marketplace and calling out to each other: 'We played the flute for you, and you did not dance; we sang a dirge, and you did not cry' " (Lk. 7:32). When the Lord identified the glory of the future, He said, "The city streets will be filled with boys and girls playing there" (Zech. 8:5).

Through play, children gain new experiences, discover new possibilities in the use of materials, develop their personalities, and think constructively. Children learn to know their own bodies—how to master and use them. They discover that arms can throw, hands can hold, and feet can walk. Whenever a child plays the role of another, he or she feels that person's situation. Sunday School lesson writers often suggest that young children play out situations to get the feeling of reality, the "you are there" quality. Why else would a teacher lead children to "march through the wilderness" or play the crowning of King Joash?

When children use blocks to build the wall of Jericho, they remember the story and learn more of what a walled city may have been. This play experience will help children more than any number of words describing the city. When children pretend to carry a basket-boat to a river and wait in the rushes for the princess, they have a sense of realism about the story of Moses. If children pretend to be tiny seeds huddled on the ground, awaiting God's sun and rain, they have deeper appreciation for God's plan for growing things. When four- or five-year-olds draw pictures of themselves helping parents, they have a better understanding of what it means to help than if they merely hear a teacher say, "We want to help at home, don't we?"

Notice, too, that children change in their play as they mature. Is a four-year-old interested in playing peek-a-boo? Why not? What are some of the toys that children leave behind as they develop? Two- and three-year-olds discard rattles, teething rings, washable books, and playpens as they are ready for wheeled toys, blocks, simple puzzles, and art materials. Play is progressive, a learning process that uses all of a child's senses.

In Sunday School, plan a variety of activities for preschoolers, all of which work toward the aim or goal of the morning. Many of these activities will look like play, but they should be carefully planned learning experiences that use eyes, ears, and many muscles in growing bodies. When two- and three-year-olds gravitate to interest centers, they should find materials that teach. Books at the book center should be chosen carefully to include some of the background needed for the Bible story. Toys and objects at each center will help accent the daily aim, and there will be teachers present to guide conversation so that it is meaningful.

You as a lone teacher do not need to struggle with the problem of planned or educational play. You do not need to determine materials nor plan all of the guided conversation, because a good Sunday School curriculum for preschoolers should provide you with an abundance of suggestions. Sunday School should be fun for preschoolers, but the fun has a purpose. It is not planned merely to entertain or "keep the children quiet." If an activity does not tie into the lesson aim, it should be reevaluated and probably discarded. Finger plays, records, art activities, playing out stories, and even helping to return materials to storage may all appear as play to the child, but you, the teacher, know better. And planning carefully for these activities is not play for you!

Guided Conversation
Guided conversation is an important teaching method

associated with educational play. What is guided conversation? It is easy to talk with a young child about a puppy, a trip to the zoo, going fishing with Daddy, or wearing new shoes. Many conversations with young children can be guided to help a child think of God. This is not easy, however! It requires a close relationship with the Lord, an understanding of children, and an awareness of the Bible content you are teaching.

Nathan had a difficult situation in kindergarten. Most of the children had trouble with Kirk, an aggressive five-year-old who bullied the children. But the teacher did not seem to realize it. Kirk was the pusher on the playground, the puncher in little unobserved ways, the tease, and the snatcher of the kindergarten room. One Sunday, Nathan related this incident about Kirk to his teacher.

"Kirk is a mean boy at our school. But know what I did? I told him his picture was the prettiest of all."

"Why, Nathan," said the teacher, "you were remembering, 'Be ye kind,' weren't you? Jesus wants us to be kind to others."

"Yep," said Nathan, very satisfied with himself. "And Kirk didn't push me that day."

This incident illustrates the guided conversation used by the teacher—and demonstrates how five-year-old Nathan was adjusting to a social situation. Only as you are in close contact with the Lord, pray about your children, and really live at the child's level will you be able to use guided conversation effectively. Notice that most Sunday School lesson writers recognize this technique and include illustrations in their lessons. Master the phrases they suggest.

Guided conversation requires a listening ear to discover where the child is in his experience and thoughts. You also need a listening heart to be ready for God to help you know what to say. "Spiritual conversation" does not consist in reviewing a Bible story or speaking in Bible verses, but it does mean being aware of God's working in your own life. If your thoughts are directed toward Him, you will find it easy to speak of Him.

I know that the phrase "guided conversation" may seem abstract at this point. We'll come to understand it better when we look in the next chapter at the interest centers where educational play takes place.

Suppose the theme for your lesson in the three-year-old department is "Jesus always sees me." This is a simple way of stating profound Biblical doctrines: God is omnipresent, and Jesus is God. Though simple, the stated truth is accurate and phrased in a way suited to twos and threes, who think egocentrically. At ten a child may say, "Jesus sees everyone." But a three-year-old sees the world solely from his point of view, and what is meaningful to him or her is, "Jesus sees *me.*"

This means that in structuring educational play you are going to select materials that can stimulate a conversation guided to your lesson aim, which is to help each child understand and sense the reality of Jesus' presence.

Let's suppose, then, that you are sitting at the book center with two or three children and one of them is looking at a page on which there's a dog. You close the book and say, "Can you see the dog now?"

"No," says the child.

You open the book and ask, "Can you see the dog now?"

"Yes," the child answers.

Then you ask, "Did you know that Jesus can see you even when you can't see Him? Jesus always sees you."

Or suppose you've placed a small ladder or step stool next to a high window. Children take turns climbing up to look out the window to see a particular flower, or tree, or bird's nest that you point out. You talk about the object, then ask "Can you see the flower now that you're off the stool?"

"No."

"Did you know that Jesus always sees you, even when you can't see Him? Isn't that wonderful?"

It is hard to estimate the impact of this kind of play-linked conversational teaching. But a true story may illustrate.

Jennifer came into the house and, obviously upset, complained to her mother: "He won't leave me alone." Mom went outside, thinking a neighbor child was teasing her three-year-old. But there was no one there, so Mom went back inside. Soon Jennifer appeared again, saying, "He won't leave me alone." Again Mom went outside, to find no one there.

After another repetition, Mom asked Jennifer, "Who won't leave you alone?" Then the story came out. Jennifer had been told not to pick her mother's flowers. Playing outside, she decided she wanted a bouquet, but when she reached out to take the flowers she remembered, "Jesus always sees me." Aware that Jesus was watching her, Jennifer couldn't bring herself to disobey her mother.

This wasn't exactly what the teacher had in mind in teaching this simple truth. I know the teacher was thinking about children who wake up at night and are afraid of the dark. What a comfort then to know that Jesus sees me, Jesus is here. But in Jennifer's case the Holy Spirit applied what she had learned to a very different situation. And Jennifer, even though she was upset at being watched, knew she couldn't do something wrong with Jesus watching and aware.

There *is* power in conversational teaching. A power that comes first from God, but also from the ways of learning that God has built into these youngest of our boys and girls.

REACT

1. What is your assessment of play? Do you regard it as something to amuse the children?

2. What experience have you had in guided conversation?

ACT

1. Continue to work on the art of guided conversation. Perhaps you are already using it more than you realize. Remember, you will not preach, but speak as naturally as you would to a friend your own age.

2. Have your children been learning through play? List some of the ways you have used it. Now read the next chapters to see how you can teach through play.

CHAPTER SEVEN
DESIGNING INTEREST CENTERS

▶The Lord Jesus taught the *multitudes* (Mk. 6:34). He taught the *small group* of 12 (Mk. 3:13, 14). He also taught the *individual*— Peter, in this instance (Mt. 18:21).

Typical Sunday School programs for preschoolers include activities for large and small groups. The Bible story, music, and worship activities are usually planned for all of the children, a large group. Then interest center or learning activities are conducted for small groups. The younger the child, the more time he or she will spend in small-group or individual activities at interest centers.

Even if your preschool teaching staff is small, you can still use interest center activities. You will need to adapt them for use with your whole group, however. Because the activities are informal, you can give attention to individuals as the rest of the children work and play.

Many small-group activities seem to be "just" play, but remember that playing is learning (see Chapter 6). The preschool teacher makes the best use of guided conversation in the small group or with an individual child. Notice in the following example how Terry's teacher used guided conversation to help Terry recognize God's care.

Terry hurried to the art table as soon as he entered the Sunday School room. "What would you like to use?" asked the teacher at this center. Without comment, three-year-old Terry took a green crayon and a large sheet of paper. Quickly he drew green grass across the bottom of the sheet. Then he selected a brown crayon and covered the paper with slashing rain. The teacher said, "Terry, tell me about your picture." As Terry described his "splashy" walk to Sunday School, the teacher made meaningful comments about God's gift of rain and our need of it.

Remember that guided conversation requires a listening ear to discover where the child is in his or her experience and thoughts. A teacher who uses guided conversation to an advantage must be a child of God who is walking in close communion with Him. If your thoughts are directed toward Him, and if you have familiarized yourself with the spiritual and mental capacities of preschoolers, you should find it easy to speak of Him in terms the child understands.

If possible, plan enough interest or learning centers to give the children a choice of activities. There must be a teacher at every center! Preschoolers need an adult to encourage them, to converse with them, and to see that they have an opportunity to use the materials. You may have any or all of the following centers, depending on your space and personnel: art, book, puzzle, block, housekeeping, music, and nature. It would be unusual to have all of these centers on any given Sunday, but you may have as many as four or five.

You will not want to set up centers or plan activities without asking yourself, "What is the purpose of this center or activity?" You must also decide what value the children will get from it and whether it is suited to the age group. Cutting, for example, is appropriate for five-year-olds but not for two-year-olds. Be sure to evaluate the activities, by asking, "What do I want the children to learn, to feel, or to experience in this activity? Is it correlated with the aim for the day?" You will also watch to see how your children respond to the various centers and activities.

Watch as the preschoolers enter their room. Most of them will be accompanied by parents and will be coming into the room one at a time. Many preschoolers give their offering as soon as they come into the room and before joining an activity; the offering may be dedicated during a worship time. Having preschoolers give their offering first is a good time-saving practice, eliminating the problem of lost coins. However, you must make the act of giving meaningful. Children do not understand if they merely deposit their coins in a box which is later emptied by a big man who comes to the door of the room. How can this money be their gift to Jesus?

Choose a container that has some relationship to the purpose of the offering. It may be a church bank or a receptacle made from a missionary curio. By all means provide a closed container so that children are not tempted to play with the coins. If you display a picture near the container it will help the children remember the reason for the offering. You do not want any child to think that he is paying his way into Sunday School. The picture may show the pastor, your church, people going into the church, a missionary supported by your church, or some object for which the money is used. A teacher should talk with the child as he or she deposits money. After giving an offering, a child is ready to choose an opening activity or learning center.

Learning centers don't *have* to be used at the beginning of your sessions. It's also possible to use centers for review. After depositing offerings, for example, children could play with blocks or dolls. Then they could sing a couple of action songs, pray, and have group time. Finally the lesson could be reviewed and reinforced as children choose to build a city wall with blocks, look at a book as part of the lesson application, or go to the nature center to develop appreciation for God's creation.

Regardless of when you use centers, they should be easily accessible to the children. Here are some centers you may wish to try:

The Nature Center
Arrange your nature center on a low table or shelf. You might include an aquarium with fish; one or more flowers or leaves; a bird's nest; a magnifying glass and small objects; a prism to refract the sunlight; a cocoon; a terrarium; and/or a variety of seeds. Vary the items, choosing those that will relate to your lesson.

The Housekeeping Center
The housekeeping center should include child-size furniture that enables preschoolers to play out what they know best in life—their own homes. Dolls, chairs, a doll bed, a stove, a cabinet-sink or stove-sink combination, and plastic dishes are good basic materials. Some teachers add dress-up clothes, modeling dough, and other materials, but no material should be provided unless it has value for the children.

As children pretend, they reveal some understanding

of how they feel in certain situations. When you suggest activities to play out at this center, you are helping children identify with some experiences that correlate with the lesson. You may suggest that the children put the dolls (and household) to bed as an activity that correlates with the Bible story of Jacob's lonely trip. If the children prepare a pretend meal and serve it, you will have opportunity to talk about thanking God for food at home. Sometimes you will sing an appropriate song, make a comment about the activity, or use a Bible verse to fit a natural home situation. Let the children enjoy "free," unstructured play much of the time, but be at hand to enter the situation when you have an opportunity to direct their thinking to the Lord.

The Music Center
The music center will not be used every week, but it is a good place to introduce new songs and provide the children with an opportunity to enjoy music. You may use a record player and the records recommended in your curriculum. Some of these will be activity records, giving the children an opportunity to move to music. Preschoolers will not sit quietly, merely listening to music without words. If you don't have a record player, try recording music on a cassette tape.

The music center may also be a good place to learn new finger plays and review old ones. In addition, four- and five-year-olds will enjoy singing familiar songs to a guitar or autoharp accompaniment. Sometimes children at this center will learn a song to sing during the large group time. This center also provides opportunity for children to experiment with rhythm band instruments.

THE HUGGABLE LEARNERS

The Book Center

Your book center will be some open shelves or perhaps a table where books are displayed. Any book chosen for this center should be judged for its teaching value. The books need not be confined to Bible stories, but they should stimulate children to develop spiritually and emotionally. Books on special subjects are always available. Consult with your Christian bookstore about books that help preschoolers, such as those that develop attitudes about God's good gifts.

While you will want many books in your department, display only a few at a time. Plan to have one book for each child who comes to this center. Be ready to look at a book with several children, remembering that two- and three-year-olds will not be patient if you read extensively. Merely commenting and questioning as you share a book with them will be enough to hold interest and direct their thinking to the Lord. All preschoolers enjoy looking at the same book more than once and hearing the same story again.

The Puzzle Center

A puzzle center interests all preschoolers. Many good, sturdy wooden puzzles are available. *Never* waste money on flimsy puzzles that do not fit well. Older primaries and juniors may patiently put together tiny or flimsy pieces, but preschoolers will not. If you are working with two- and three-year-olds, provide some puzzles with only three or four pieces. Five-year-olds can work puzzles with six to eight pieces or more. Establish some rules at the puzzle center:
1. We do not throw pieces.
2. We work with only one puzzle at a time.
3. We sit far enough away from the next person so that the pieces do not get mixed.

4. We return one puzzle before taking another.

If you do not have a puzzle rack, designate a shelf where puzzles are to be kept.

The Block Center

The block center will be a very popular place with many preschoolers. They need opportunities to construct, to put things together, to build. A toddler needs sturdy, lightweight cardboard blocks, but you will want to supply wooden blocks for three-, four-, and five-year-olds. Hollow wooden blocks are useful because they come in big sizes and can be used to build things a child can use—steps, a wall, a train, or a boat. Hardwood blocks are expensive, but they are durable and safe. They will last many years with good care and occasional refinishing.

The Art Center

Art center activities are often *expressional*, encouraging children to express what they have learned. Some curriculum offers art as one of several activities to use in helping children show how they could apply the lesson. Another course may suggest the same art activity for all children in the small groups. Still another curriculum may consider "art" the printed handwork project which a child completes according to directions.

You will want to vary materials and methods at the art center. Do not think of crayons as the only medium for preschoolers, but experiment with clay, paint, chalk, and freehand cutting and pasting.

Do not be discouraged if your children are hesitant to use some art materials. If they have not used a material before, they may well be hesitant. Talk with them about the material and demonstrate how to use it. If children ask you to draw their pictures for them, talk with them about the object to be drawn: "What color is your house? What color of dog are you thinking about? Where do you think the wheels on the truck belong?" Do not draw for the children, because you will deny them the joy of personal achievement. Do not go over a child's work to show him or her what should have been drawn or what color should have been used. You are not teaching art; you are using art to help children express what they have learned.

Crayons

With kindergarten crayons (largest size available) and large sheets of paper, two-year-olds can color freely. Newsprint or smooth sheets of wrapping paper will be satisfactory. The children may work at a table, on the floor, or draw on paper fastened to a wall.

How does a child move from mere motion to meaning? At first the young child seems to attack the paper with the crayon, holding the crayon in a tight grip to make uncontrolled lines we call scribbles. Later the child uses the crayon in almost a rhythmic motion, repeating the same design, but using a variety of colors.

As children mature physically and mentally, they have better control over crayons. They begin to give their pictures names, and their art may have recognizable meaning. We can see this stage in the work of some three-year-olds, most four-year-olds and nearly all five-year-olds. When children are about four, they begin to be selective in colors and prefer to draw something that has meaning for them. Notice that colors have meaning for children, but they may not be the traditional meanings. One day some four-year-olds were drawing "big" things God made. There was ecstasy on her face as Frannie drew a purple maple!

Once children are capable of recognizable pictures, they will grow in their ability to portray ideas. They draw things as they appear to children, sometimes including not only what they see but what they know should be in the picture. They may draw the interior of a house and try to include all the furniture. Usually the object that is most important to a child will be the largest. You may, for example, see very small shepherds worshiping a large baby Jesus.

Clay

Clay (or modeling dough for twos and threes, who usually find clay too stiff) is a good medium for young children. It does not require coordination of the smaller muscles, and preschoolers enjoy pounding, punching, thumping, rolling, and pulling it. You will seldom use clay for a take-home project, but this medium provides ample opportunity for expression.

Do not expect the children to make something immediately. The first stages of clay work are handling and experimenting. You may need to show children how to make a shape or develop a form. Once the children have seen your work and understand it, roll the clay back into a ball; you do not want to stifle creativity or invite frustration by providing a model.

When you make clay available, provide vinyl place mats or 12-inch square boards, such as corrugated cardboard, to use on a newspaper-covered table. You must also provide clean-up facilities. If you have only a few children working with clay, a nearby washroom will be adequate. But if more than six children are using clay, you may want to invest in some of the premoistened tissues now available.

You will find a variety of clays and modeling doughs on the market, or you may make your own flour-and-salt dough. Even though the dough or clay keeps for some time in airtight containers, do not use it too long, because it picks up dirt and germs. Vary the color of the clay, but explain that colors are not to be mixed. Do not expect a child to mold recognizable objects. Some children may, but others will not succeed in making an object that you can identify. For this reason, many teachers consider clay one of the least valuable activities.

Paint

Using paints will make more work for you, teacher, but the children will enjoy this medium and profit from it. You will not want to use painting every Sunday, but you may offer several opportunities during the year to do finger painting, spatter painting (rubbing a paint-dipped toothbrush across a window-screen frame over paper), easel painting, or printmaking.

Printmaking may provide a new experience for many of your preschoolers. In printmaking, the child presses an object into tempera paint and then onto a sheet of paper. The object may be a bottle cap, a bit of sponge, a napkin ring, or something else. Unless you demonstrate more than once, children doing print-making for the first time have a tendency to use the object as they would a brush, scrubbing back and forth in an attempt to cover the paper. These children are not stupid; they are merely trying to use a new object in an old way.

Painting requires adequate preparation, including telling parents that children will be painting in Sunday School. If parents know you plan to use this medium, they will dress their children in washable clothing. Parents can also supply smocks or aprons for their children. You must have adequate clean-up facilities for painting—a nearby washroom or a large basin of water and towels.

Preschoolers should never be asked to paint with the small brushes and boxes of paint used by elementary pupils. The types of painting described here are the methods that preschoolers can use satisfactorily.

Though painting is a valuable learning activity, you will want to evaluate its use for your children. Use the questions given in the first section of this chapter to help you evaluate its use in your situation. Then be sure that you have time, space, smocks, understanding parents, and the materials for painting. Finger painting and easel painting may not be activities for you. But most preschool departments can manage spatter painting and printmaking.

Cutting and Pasting

Preschool children cannot cut out small figures, but four- and five-year-olds can try tearing shapes, such as leaves to add to trees, or flowers for a garden. When you are teaching a child to cut, draw straight lines for cutting, then circles, and then more difficult outlines. Do not criticize a child if he or she does not cut on the lines; leave this for the public school teacher to perfect. But do provide preschoolers with scissors that have round safety ends, not the sharp-pointed ones the children will choose if given a choice. Do not waste money on plastic scissors, because they will not cut paper. Always test scissors before you purchase them.

Preschoolers from age three on will enjoy pasting. The younger children are not ready for cutting, but they can paste in place what you provide. It will take time for three-year-olds to learn that they need only a small dab of paste. Set out what each child needs on a small piece of paper.

THE HUGGABLE LEARNERS

Any art activity should be the child's own work. If you have to do most of the work on a project, it is too difficult for preschoolers and is not a good learning experience for them. Remember that when young children paint pictures, draw with crayons, or make clay objects, they are not creating art. They are setting down their impressions. Because preschoolers cannot write and many are still struggling to verbalize, encourage art as a means of expressing what they have learned or how they feel as a result of what you have taught.

Interest Centers Are for Teaching
The major thing to remember is that your interest centers are for teaching—not traditional teaching, but the conversational kind of teaching described in the last chapter. This means that each week you need to have available at your centers those materials which can be related to your lesson aim. Put away materials which do not fit. Work together with the rest of the department staff to plan ways to direct the children's play and thought to the truth which the day's lesson is intended to impress. There's no need to deprive boys and girls of fun, or of the opportunity to move freely among the interest centers. But never let the children lose the meaning through the fun of doing.

REACT
1. Do you agree that preschoolers need both large- and small-group activities? Why? Does your answer include the fact that preschoolers learn through their senses?

2. If communicating God's Word to little children is important, are small-group activities too great an effort for you to undertake? Why not?

ACT

1. What interest or learning centers are you using now?

2. What centers are suggested in your curriculum? Remember, if the activities are suggested without being set up at a center, the curriculum is recognizing and advising the small-group learning activities.

3. If the learning centers or activities themselves are not suggested in your curriculum, what should you do?

4. If you have not been using the learning activities described in this chapter, which one are you planning to try first? Try it soon!

CHAPTER EIGHT
PREPARING YOUR ROOM

▶We know that children learn better and are happier in an accepting and caring environment. You could follow every suggestion in this chapter for rooms and materials but not provide the caring, loving environment that will help children love God and His Word. You make the difference! Strive for the best facilities, materials, and methods, but do not lose sight of the fact that the children will learn most from you and your relationship to the Lord. This is something preschoolers can see, hear, and feel emotionally.

Now that you know more about the people you are to teach and how you are to teach them, you are ready to think about where you will teach. What is an ideal room for preschoolers? How can you adapt to a less than ideal situation? How big a room do you need? What is the best shape for a room? What should be in a room for preschoolers? Is it possible to have either too much or too little furniture? How many children belong in one room?

First, take a look at your Preschool Departments. Ideally you will have a separate room for two-year-olds, one for three-year-olds, and perhaps one room for four- and five-year-olds.

Two-year-olds: An ideal room for two-year-olds will have thirty-five square feet of space for each child. This is child space. It does not include the space occupied by storage areas or large equipment.

Three-year-olds: About fifteen three-year-olds may be grouped in one room—no more than ten or twelve two-year-olds in one room. Use the same space allotment for three-year-olds.

Fours and fives: Four- and five-year-olds may be in separate rooms or in one room. Limit the group to no more than twenty or twenty-five children and provide thirty square feet of space for each child. These figures express the ideal, of course, but they will give you a standard to work toward.

If you were to plan the ideal arrangement, you would provide a separate room for each age. The rooms would be slightly more rectangular than square in shape, because such floor space is more adaptable to arranging and rearranging interest centers, play space, and an area for all the children to gather together for the Bible story and worship activities. Each room would include a water supply, and rest rooms (including a toilet low enough for easy use by preschoolers) would be nearby.

If you do not have the ideal situation, keep adapting the space you have to create the best possible environment for preschoolers. Keeping your local building codes and the requirements for good rooms before you, continue to make as many adaptations, changes, and improvements as possible. If you cannot do everything this year, set up a five-year improvement program. Check your rooms against the following list.

THE HUGGABLE LEARNERS

1. All preschool rooms should be on the ground level, not in the basement!
2. Provide floor coverings, including rugs, that are smooth, durable, and easily cleaned.
3. Be sure that all window and door areas are completely safe.
4. Cover any hot pipes or radiators in your room, and insert protective coverings over all low electrical outlets.
5. Provide adequate heat and light.
6. Keep the room clean. Preschoolers spend more time on the floor than do any other groups in your Sunday School.
7. Paint the room a bright color that appeals to children.

If you really want to evaluate a preschool room, take time to remove all the furniture. Now take a look at the room, the windows, the walls, and the floor covering. Before replacing anything, decide what you like and do not like about the room. Will a fresh coat of paint help? New curtains? A different floor covering? What can you afford to do first?

Take one more look at the walls before you replace any of the furniture. What is on them? Are there pictures that appeal to children? Pictures, bulletin boards, coat hooks, a picture rail—anything children need to see or use—should be at a child's eye level. Don't guess about a child's eye level, but plan to measure the exact height the next time you have one of the children in the room. If children are to learn, the environment must help them.

Now begin replacing the furniture, evaluating each piece. Do not return any piece unless it serves a purpose and is the proper size for the age group involved; a preschool room is not the place for cast-off furniture.

Chairs and tables are important. The chairs should have seats ten or twelve inches from the floor. A good table will be sturdy, have an easily cleaned surface, and measure ten inches higher than the seats of the chairs used at the table. If you do not have space for both tables and chairs, sacrifice the chairs, because your preschoolers will not mind standing as they work at the tables.

Do you have adequate shelving for books, puzzles, and toys? Where are the blocks stored? Shelves are good storage space for the large hollow wooden blocks or for the lightweight cardboard blocks. A box is the best place for smaller wooden blocks.

Arrange your rooms so that they do not look cluttered. If possible, use a nearby hallway or room for the children's coatroom. Parents can help children there, leaving more space in your room. If you want to control entrance and exit of children, you could cut the door to your room in half horizontally so that both halves open and close independently of each other; this type of door is often called a dutch door. You could open the top of the door to deliver two- or three-year-olds to their parents, who will take them to the outdoor wrap area.

After you have provided the essentials, you are ready to add other items that make the environment more pleasant. Just be sure you have room for them. Additional items for the learning centers are described in Chapter 7. A piano, coatrack for adults, an adult rocker, or desk would be welcome additions to your room if you have the space. Perhaps you feel that a piano is essential. It is a good piece of equipment, but preschoolers will sing just as well without accompaniment or with an autoharp or guitar. You set the stage for a good learning experience when you carefully plan for the equipment that meets the needs of your pupils. Unless children are going to make use of the equipment, is it worth having in the room?

All preschool workers want to achieve the ideal, but few will. Probably the most important need for your children is space—to move, to play out stories, and to learn through activities. But even if your space is limited, remember that you are the one who can help the children learn. Plan for improved conditions in the future, but realize that you set the atmosphere for learning by the interesting things you have in the room and the varied activities you plan for the children.

Learning Materials
Because children learn through doing—involving touching, seeing, and hearing—there should be plenty of materials for them to use. Provide pictures, puppets, objects and models, flannel boards and figures for them, flash cards, dioramas, flip charts, bulletin boards, and all of the materials used in the small-group activities or interest centers described in Chapter 7. Your curriculum materials will help you learn about many of these teaching aids. Some of them are available from your Christian bookstore or Sunday School supplier, and others you will want to make yourself.

Pictures help enrich the experiences of all children. They are a valuable resource. Prepared picture sets are often a part of curriculum materials, but you will also want to collect other pictures from magazines, newspapers, display materials, catalogs, calendars, church literature, discarded picture books, and school supply houses.

Use these guidelines in selecting pictures. Use good-quality, clear, large pictures with few details. Show a picture of one elephant, for example, rather than a herd of them. Trim the picture carefully and mount it on a harmonizing shade of construction paper and then on poster board or cardboard. Investigate some of the newer processes available through art stores, such as laminating a picture that will be handled frequently or dry mounting pictures for longer-lasting adhesion. When you use a picture, be sure that all the children can see it, even if this means taking turns. Preschoolers will enjoy pictures that have people in them.

It is impossible to list all of the teaching aids available, but here are some of the most worthwhile:

Flannel boards may be homemade or purchased. You can buy flannel board figures or make your own figures to illustrate the Bible story. Preschoolers will be happy with simple chenille-wire figures, or you may find figures in old Sunday School papers or Bible coloring books. Try to have all figures for one story in proportion to one another. Paste scraps of felt, suede, flannel, or sandpaper to the backs of the figures.

Flip charts are made from chart paper or lightweight cardboard. Use one picture on a sheet to illustrate one idea in a Bible verse or song. Most preschoolers cannot read, so you need not include any words.

Puppets are good to use in telling a story, or the puppets may act out the story. A puppet may encourage children to put away supplies or come to the Bible story area. Investigate available puppets and check to see how your curriculum recommends using them. Simple puppets can be made from clothes pins or chenille wires (pipe cleaners).

Bulletin boards are used to display pictures, seasonal objects, children's art, and teaching exhibits.

Dioramas are best suited to older preschoolers,

because the figures are small and the scenes may be complicated. A diorama is a three-dimensional scene placed in a box that is set on its side. The figures, cut from pictures, are mounted to stand in front of the background.

Sand tables also make ideal settings for storytelling.

Your children will want to touch many of the objects that you bring. Touching is a way of learning for the preschooler, so do not take objects or pictures to Sunday School unless you expect the children to handle them.

Is Yours a Balanced Program?
Now that you have read about the parts of the Sunday School hour—the teaching methods used most often, and the room, furnishings, and atmosphere—you can better evaluate your program. Is your whole hour meeting the children's needs, or the teachers' convenience? Every preschool teacher is constantly striving to keep things in balance—large- and small-group activities, quiet and active times, listening and doing—and to reinforce the familiar while introducing new concepts. No two sessions will be exactly alike, but there will be planned variety. You are never engaged in activity for the sake of activity, but are constantly teaching new words and ideas, and giving new experiences to your children.

Teaching preschoolers is work, but it is worth all the effort you put into it. Remember, yours is a rare privilege—the opportunity of teaching young children about the Lord and leading them to love Him and serve Him.

REACT
1. How many opportunities are there in the average

Sunday School session for a child to worship? For example, a child is watching the rain beat against the windowpane, and you say, "Thank You, God, for rain, which makes things grow." How many opportunities for worship are you using?

2. If you are going to teach children through their senses—not just their listening ears—you will spend many hours searching for the materials you need. Is this worth the time?

ACT

1. If you are a wise teacher, you will plan ahead. Go through your manual when you first receive it. Note the Bible content, planning to study it in your own personal devotions. Then make a list of the materials you will want to collect and use: nature objects, pictures, items for a tabletop scene, etc.

2. Involve others in helping you. Preschool teachers probably need more materials than any other teachers in the Sunday School. Ask senior citizens to cut and mount pictures for you. Invite teenagers to sort papers, prepare bulletin boards, or help in other ways.

Make a list of the jobs that someone else could do to help you prepare learning materials. Now pray that the Lord will lead you to the person who can be your helper behind the scenes.

CHAPTER NINE
A TEAM
MINISTRY

▶"Each one should use whatever gift he has received to serve others, faithfully administering God's grace in its various forms" (I Pet. 4:10).

Teaching preschoolers is a team ministry. As a teaching team, members of a Preschool Department staff use a variety of skills, and in a variety of ways they are dispensers of God's wonderfully varied grace. On other, older age levels, teaching may be a transaction involving one teacher with a small class of learners. For many reasons, this is neither effective nor desirable with preschoolers.

Often preschoolers require individual attention. An accident happens; a child becomes upset and strikes out at others; another is overcome with sudden homesickness and needs comforting. Such incidents make it important that enough staff members be present to show the personal attention so important to giving younger children a sense of warmth and security.

But preschool staff members are teachers as well as comforters. The individualized, interest-center teaching and the conversational teaching approach that fill play activities with meaning require that enough staff members relate to little clusters of children. This informal time is prime teaching time; it demands staff members who are trained and who have a thorough understanding of the ways preschoolers are to be taught and the ways they learn.

Perhaps even more important, however, is that each preschool staff member adds something of the warmth of his or her own personality to the learning experience. *Who we are* as persons who love Jesus and who love the children does come through to children. As preschoolers learn to trust their teachers and sense the security of their love, this attitude of trust and security helps provide the foundations of a growing faith in Christ discussed in Chapters 1 and 2.

What's important in helping a staff become a team, a *team* that teaches, rather than simply a group of individuals who teach?

Staff Roles

A variety of roles are important in the department team, and can be filled by one or several of the staff. Each teacher, of course, is first of all a friend who has concern for each child and finds opportunity to show it, from the first step into the room, on through individualized and group activities, to the final, warm good-bye at the end of the hour. Each teacher on the preschool staff needs to relate to the children as individual personalities; relating to them in a group is far less important at this early age.

Each teacher also will be called on for conversational teaching at the interest and activity centers. This means each will need to know how to use play as a teaching medium (rather than simply supervising free play). It also means that each teacher will need to understand thoroughly the content and teaching strategy of each class hour. It's not enough for only the department superintendent or "master teacher" to tell the Bible story and for the rest of the staff simply to be there to supervise the children. As we've seen, every part of the preschool class hour is a teaching activity. Songs, prayer, and play are as much part of the Bible teaching impact of preschool ministry as the story itself is.

While each staff member does have teaching ministry roles, there are additional special roles that need to be filled. "Story lady" (or man) is an important one. The storyteller needs to understand preschoolers' short attention span, tell the story with warmth and interest, and use the many aids that can help make Bible story time a fascinating one for children.

One of the staff can also take responsibility for songs during worship time, or—in the case of two- and three-year-olds—each teacher should be ready to sing the simple, repetitive teaching songs that come with a good curriculum.

The division of labor made possible by the variety of roles in teaching preschoolers means that individuals with special talents and skills can use them to make unique contributions. The best storyteller on the team can accept this special role; special talents in preparation of interest centers or other projects can be used.

In addition, consider the importance of including both male and female role models for your preschoolers. In an age when so many children grow up in single-parent homes, it's worth the effort to recruit couples and men as well as women. Grandparents and dads, for example, can fit into and make distinctive contributions to the teaching team.

As you recruit staff members, be sure you know them. Today's sensitivity to the problems of child abuse and molestation require reasonable caution. For example, it is best to have at least two adult helpers in the room at any time.

It is important, then, to always think of the department staff as a team, not as separate and individual teachers. And it's important to take definite steps to make sure the staff functions as a team!

Unified Understanding

What elements go into building a staff into a team? One of the most important is a common purpose and understanding of preschool ministry. The issues addressed in this book—goals in teaching, how preschoolers learn, impact of various teaching methods, structure of the hour and the room—are all important foundations of effective team performance.

Within the framework provided by general principles, however, many specific and shared plans need to be developed. All on the teaching team need to understand the goals of the unit and the weekly individual lessons. The team should talk over the needs of individuals in the department and plan ways to use the curriculum objectives to meet specific needs. Interest centers should be discussed and planned by the team, with each individual understanding how each play activity contributes toward reaching the objectives of the session and unit. Teaching songs correlated with the unit should be learned by all as well. Often special decorations for the room, or special activity projects suggested in the curriculum, will need to be planned.

This kind of coordination demands that the team hold regular planning meetings. While normally these will not be needed weekly, each new unit of lessons clearly demands a staff get-together.

What happens when a staff gets together to plan for a

coming unit? Here's an outline of a possible approach to such a meeting.

Unit Planning Meeting

7:30—7:50   Sharing, evaluation of last unit
     Emphasis on growth of individuals observed

7:50—8:10   Preview of Bible content, goals, and objectives of upcoming unit and individual lessons (by superintendent or storyteller)

8:10—8:40   Preview of suggested interest-center or play-learning activities.
     Generation of additional ideas, modifications in view of department resources, space, etc.

8:40—8:50   Learning of correlated songs

8:50—9:00   Planning of special roles or tasks

9:00—9:30   Discussion of special needs of individual children, especially in view of upcoming unit. Pray for the children about the truths being taught.

This kind of planning meeting will be most meaningful if each staff member has a teacher's manual and studies it before the meeting. It will also be helpful if the superintendent prepares for each teacher a statement of unit and lesson objectives and ties these in with the overall goals specified in Chapter 4 of this book.

While the unit planning meeting is a very important gathering for the staff, other kinds of staff meetings are also important. If a unit of lessons extends beyond four weeks, to six or seven weeks, an evaluation session in

A TEAM MINISTRY

the middle of the unit would be important. These mid-unit meetings give opportunity for exploring different areas of the department's ministry as well as the practical, day-to-day operation of the team. Here's a typical mid-unit meeting outline. Notice that it stresses staff sharing and problem solving and focusing on individual children in the department.

Mid-unit Planning Meeting

7:30—8:00   Sharing, evaluation of progress in unit. Discussion of problems, plans for solution.

8:00—8:20   Discussion of individual children. Development of a staff anecdotal record (each individual contributes observations, information on each child, to build together a better understanding of deeper concern for him).

8:20—9:20   Special project study

9:20—9:30   Prayer time

What might a "special project" be? Anything dealing with the general effectiveness of the department's ministry. For instance, you might work together on a plan for visiting the families, providing a resource sheet to help parents continue your teaching thrust at home. Or you might work on decorating your room or preparing some special object for an interest center. Or you might have a report on a book on teaching preschoolers. You might view a film or have a preschool teacher from the public school talk about discipline problems and how to handle them effectively.

Your special projects studies will grow out of the needs you and the staff observe in your local situation. If regular staff meetings are a feature of your preschool

99

ministry, you'll find a growing number of areas becoming "special interest" concerns of your staff! And you'll need time like this to deal with them.

Regular staff get-togethers are utterly necessary if the staff members are to grow into a functioning teaching team. To the extent that all your staff members share a common philosophy of teaching and learning and work together to plan and carry out unit and weekly programs, a team spirit will be developed. Developing the staff into a team may take many months. But this concern is a priority for those seeking to have a quality ministry with the young children who are invited to come to Jesus.

Common Spiritual Concern

There's more to staff meetings than program planning and more to team effectiveness than individual teaching skills. A common spiritual concern, a unity of spirit, a fellowship of love on the team, are vital ingredients of every Christian relationship, and especially of the relationship of those engaged in common ministry.

The spiritual dimension is demonstrated in two areas, both of which emphasize Jesus' own concern for persons: A team with a common spiritual concern has learned, first, to care about each other and, second, to care about the children as individuals.

Staff times together need to reflect growing concern of the members for each other. Note that in the meeting plans, time is always given for sharing. If anything, the suggested times for this vital interaction are too short! In many churches, fellowship or sharing time precedes the planning meetings. A meal together in one of the homes; a time for studying Scripture together; time to pray with and for each other—these are all important dimensions of the staff's team life.

Particularly when a staff is just forming, special times to get to know one another are important. The deepening of prayer fellowship over the months of shared ministry will bring constantly greater depth to the relationship—and to the ministry.

Getting to know the children as individual personalities is another vital aspect of developing spiritual concern. Our ministry of teaching is a ministry to individuals, each of whom is important and precious to God. We come to appreciate the importance of each and share increasingly in God's love for each individual by coming to know each one better.

One way to increase knowing is by keeping team or staff anecdotal records. Each time you get together as a staff, spend some time discussing individual preschoolers. Share what each of the staff has observed during class. If you've been in the home or know the home, add to your record home background information. These records are kept to enable you to see progress as each child develops through his year(s) with the department, and they help staff members see each child as a unique individual. Prayer for the children as individuals and for special needs they may have will further deepen the spiritual concern that marks teachers who share Christ's love for the young.

Sometimes pairing of staff members into visitation teams can serve a dual purpose of helping the staff come to know each other better and get a better insight into individuals and their families. Whenever there are special tasks to accomplish, if two or more of the staff can be asked to work together, you'll increase the opportunity for staff involvement with each other in a spiritually significant way.

In everything, be sensitive to the personal dimensions of your ministry, the personal relationships within the staff, and a personal concern for preschoolers. This concern will grow as your children are increasingly seen as individuals to be loved for themselves, and who are led to trust and know your staff members and the Lord you represent.

REACT

1. In what ways does your present staff function as a team? In what ways does it need to grow in its team unity?

2. Beside the name of each teacher in your department, list his or her special abilities or talents. How does he or she fit into the team? What abilities could be better used?

ACT

1. Schedule a team unit-planning meeting for the next unit, and work through with the other staff members just what you'll want to accomplish then.

2. Begin anecdotal records on each child in your department.

CHAPTER TEN
REACHING INTO THE HOME

▶"These commandments that I give you today are to be upon your hearts. Impress them on your children. Talk about them when you sit at home and when you walk along the road, when you lie down and when you get up" (Deut. 6:6, 7).

The primary communicators of faith to preschoolers are their parents. This is God's order, and it has never been superseded.

This does not, of course, reduce the importance of the church's ministry to preschoolers. Instead it establishes the church's ministry as an adjunct and supplement to the home, not as a substitute or supplanter. At the same time, it increases the importance of the church's preschool ministry by showing the potential for extending that ministry through the week by aiding parents in their teaching tasks!

When we think about helping parents teach preschoolers, we need to do several things. We need to review the nature of teaching as it applies to preschoolers. We need to look at the problems facing parents. And we need to realize the resources we can provide to parents.

THE HUGGABLE LEARNERS

First, as discussed in earlier chapters, we need to remember that teaching preschoolers is a part of nurture. The word *nurture* implies growth, development. It speaks of a process, not of a product. No ministry to preschoolers can, in itself, produce spiritually mature adults. The capacity for maturity—be it physical, social, emotional, or spiritual—awaits growth into adulthood. So our teaching of preschoolers is not focused on the product. It is focused on supplying what is needed for the *process of growth to proceed normally and healthily.*

In earlier chapters, we've seen that preschoolers need a relational context in which they feel loved and secure if they are to grow as open, trusting persons. We've seen some of the basic Bible concepts they need to build into their understanding of life and reality: truths about who God and Jesus are, and that the Bible is God's Book. We've also seen some of the simple attitudes and behaviors we want to foster, encouraging them at the earliest ages to begin responding to God with loving obedience.

It is very important to realize that such learning involves not merely information but *being*. Jesus told His followers, "Everyone who is fully trained will *be like* his teacher" (Lk. 6:40, italics added). *Being* is the focus of Christian teaching, and children learn and become like their teachers. A primary focus, then, of ministry to preschoolers is on providing relationships for them with adults who do love and obey God, and who will be the right kind of models for these littlest disciples.

Parents as Models
As a teacher ministering in Sunday School or children's church, you are a model for the preschoolers you teach.

104

But the *primary model* remains their parents, the adults with whom they spend most of their waking hours.

What do parents need to be good models for their preschoolers? Deuteronomy 6 points out that the parents need to take God's Word to heart, to make it a living part of their own lives and personalities. Then they need to talk about God and His words in the process of daily living. The truths on adults' hearts need to be shared with their children.

What is important, then, is not that the parents know everything about the Bible or try to teach everything about the Bible at home, but that they grow in their relationship with Jesus; that they demonstrate His love and trustworthiness in their family; that, as they live daily with their children, they talk about God and His place in the family's life. This simple pattern of *lived faith* is critical during the early years of a child's life: it lays the foundation for his or her future life with God and with other people.

Parents need to understand preschool teaching as *being*—and build into their lives ways and times to express their faith simply and with meaning.

This brief insight into home training of preschoolers helps us understand many of the problems facing parents. Most problems hinge on a failure to grasp the developmental nature of preschoolers' nurture and a lack of information as to how parents can make the most significant contributions to their children's spiritual growth. We often have teacher-training emphases, but parent training has historically been neglected by the church. Noting this, we can see one immediate answer to the question of how we can help parents. We can help parents by getting them to better understand their teaching ministry! Chapters 1, 4, 5, and 7 in this book would be particularly helpful in this regard; insights given here into preschool ministry are just those that parents (as well as church staff teachers) need to know!

Strategies for Helping Parents

How else could we help parents better understand the nature of their nurturing ministry with preschoolers?

1. We might invite small groups of parents to meet in different teachers' homes for "insight" sessions.
2. We might encourage parents to read books like this one and *Parents: Round-the-Clock Teachers* (David C. Cook Publishing Co., 1988). The latter is especially written for parents.
3. We might develop and send home monthly newsletters, using excerpts from this and similar books as part of the content (after getting permission from the publishers, of course).
4. We might divide the families among staff members, and have teams of two teachers each visit the homes to explain the department's goals and philosophy.
5. We might encourage a mother's club for sharing ideas and talking over common problems and concerns.
6. We might encourage parents to visit Sunday School for several consecutive Sundays, limiting the number present to no more than two couples.
7. We might pay special attention to the needs of single parents, because raising toddlers alone can be extremely stressful and exhausting. We could befriend these parents and provide extra nurture for their preschoolers.

Each of these approaches is a costly one in terms of time and effort. It involves asking a staff to go the second mile (and even a third!) in an already demanding ministry. But this kind of ministry *to the home* is of vital importance to the future of the children you have come to know and care for.

It is true, of course, that the most basic need of the home—for parents to be growing Christians—probably cannot be met by the preschool staff. Parents will need to be involved with other ministries of the church—adult classes, the worship services, perhaps small home Bible study and prayer groups—as a source for their own feeding and development. Yet the friendship and encouragement of staff members can provide a source of mutual fellowship and encouragement.

Contact with the home is particularly needed if the parents are not yet Christians. When visiting a non-Christian home, it's important that you approach contacts with a clear vision of your purpose. While your long-range goal is to draw the adults to Christ and thus lay the foundation for a truly Christian home, a direct, or "hard-sell," evangelism is seldom best. Non-Christians need not only to hear the Gospel presented, they need to see the reality of Jesus in His disciples!

To build a relationship with non-Christians in which the reality of Jesus is communicated, you must assume that they are interested (with you) in the spiritual growth of their children. (After all, they are bringing or permitting their children to be in your department!) You also need to realize that God loves them *as they are*, and that it is your place to love them as He does (cf. Mt. 5:43-48). As they come to feel confident in your love and concern for them, their defenses will be lowered, and they will be open to exploring Jesus' claims.

This "gentle evangelism" approach will not, of course, be one you will take in every situation. When you meet a passing stranger, there is hardly time for development of a relationship. Then, if God leads, a direct presentation of the Gospel is fitting. But when you have built-in points of continuing contact, as through a child in your department, the gentle approach is nearly always the right one. As you express Jesus' love for parents and child, doors will open for you or others to share Jesus Himself, and hearts will be readied for that message.

Thus far, then, we've noted two needs of parents and ways that the preschool staff can be used by God to minister to them. First, Christian nurture demands Christians! And God can use you to build relationships with adults through which they may be led to Christ and their growth encouraged. While evangelism and nurture of adults may not be the primary responsibility of the preschool staff, each contribution in these areas is vital to the overall development of the children you teach.

Second, parents do need to understand the principles of nurture on which preschool ministry is based. This educational task *is* a primary responsibility of preschool departments. Understanding the nature of preschool ministry better than any other group in the church, you will want to share your understanding with moms and dads.

Providing Parental Resources
There is another important way you can help parents. Not only can you help them grasp principles; you can provide resources to enrich home teaching. Many of these resources are the very ones you develop for your in-class teaching.

1. *Bible story pictures* can be pinned next to a child's bed for nighttime conversation and reminders.

2. *Teaching songs* used in church can be supplied to parents, to be sung with children during the week. Be sure to get publishers' permission before copying words or music, however.

3. *Take-home papers* provided with most curriculum can be read and talked about in the home.

4. *Interest-center* activities, involving children in play that uses many of the senses, can be communicated to parents as units are launched. Parents can be shown how to involve their children in similar play at home and how to teach them conversationally.

5. A *bulletin board* in the kitchen or *art projects* taped to the refrigerator can be suggested to hold Sunday or at-home handwork.

6. *Family activities* may flow naturally from upcoming lessons. Would a nature walk, a visit to the store, or a trip to the zoo relate to what preschoolers learn in Sunday School? These and many other simple activities can be done together, with spontaneous moments for prayer or worship or talking about God.

7. The child's *memory verse*, added to other verses the family might be learning, can be repeated nightly at the supper table.

8. *Books* from the church library or a local Christian bookstore can be recommended and used.

9. *Craft projects*, such as collages, can be completed as parents and children work together.

This ministry of providing resources is a very practical, powerful way to enrich the homelives of your preschoolers. There are a number of avenues through which to communicate these resources: home visits, parent visits and observations of class, weekly take-home papers, newsletters, spontaneous contacts made with parents while shopping, parents' club meetings, and more.

Of these, the newsletter is probably one of the most powerful yet easiest to do. All it takes is an editor (one of your department staff or a special recruit to major in home ministry coordination) and a little effort.

What might go into such a newsletter? When should it be mailed? Normally, a newsletter might be sent at the beginning of each unit of lessons. For extra-long units, it could be distributed monthly. Typical contents might include the following:

1. A statement of unit and lesson aims as developed in the unit planning meetings (see Chapter 9). Bible passages used should be incorporated here.
2. A column suggesting things to do with children at home to reinforce the teaching. Interest center activities can be described with conversational teaching hints.
3. Songs used with the unit (including the tunes) are another possible feature. Be sure to get the publisher's permission.
4. A book report, highlighting a specific idea or concept that provides instant help.
5. News of children and families. Chatty items, what little Meredith or Jeremy said in class, a good idea shared at a mothers' club meeting, etc.
6. A short, aimed-at-adults devotional based on the passages to be used with the children.

These and many other features will find their way into department newsletters and build the church and the home into a coordinated ministry unit.

And this is really what we need. It is not a matter of the church *or* the home in ministry to preschoolers. It is a matter of the church working *with* the home! These are two powerful avenues that God has given us to touch young lives for time and eternity with the gentle, yet lasting mark of Jesus Christ. Either of these avenues is incomplete alone. Young children need to learn at home from their moms and dads. And young children need to learn with each other, in a setting where other adults model and teach the reality of Jesus and the importance of God's Book. And in each of these settings, home and church, young children deserve the *best* Christian nurture we can provide!

In a very real way, the effectiveness of nurture in both these settings does depend on the preschool staff. Because you are an organized team, trained to understand and minister to these youngest of children, it is likely that you will have unique expertise to equip moms and dads for their ministries. As you grow in your understanding of your ministry and in your skill as a team, you will be able to communicate to parents what you know and are learning.

Because you have a planned teaching program in your curriculum, you will be able to coordinate the learning in each home. So it *is* up to you to take the lead. It *is* up to you to enrich the homelife of your preschoolers, as well as to provide a context for spiritual growth on Sunday mornings.

And how wonderful an opportunity this is! God *is* at work in the lives of even these younger children. The foundations of faith *are* being laid.

May God use you increasingly to provide the firmest of foundations—and to open up the future of these tiny ones to the fullness of His love and transforming power.

REACT
1. How important do you feel the home is in the life of

111

a preschooler? Can you see evidence of its importance in the lives of those you teach now?

2. How many parents of those in your department do you believe are aware of principles of nurture discussed in this book? How many are using teaching tools to coordinate their ministry at home with what you teach Sundays?

ACT

1. Work as a team to create a parents' newsletter. What items would you want to include? Divide up responsibilities and see how long it takes to develop an issue of this powerful parent aid.

2. Discuss with other members of your preschool staff what goals you want to set for helping parents. What do you see as needs? How might these needs best be met? Write out specific objectives.

3. Determine how you will work to reach the objectives you spelled out above. Pray about what God wants you to do together in this vital, yet demanding, dimension of your ministry to preschoolers.